Developing Effective
Special Educators

Developing Effective Special Educators

Building Bridges Across the Profession

Alice Tesch Graham

Gia Anselmo Renaud

Martha McCann Rose

TEACHERS COLLEGE PRESS

TEACHERS COLLEGE | COLUMBIA UNIVERSITY

NEW YORK AND LONDON

Published by Teachers College Press,® 1234 Amsterdam Avenue, New York, NY 10027

Copyright © 2020 by Teachers College, Columbia University

Library of Congress Control Number: 2020939002

ISBN 978-0-8077-6414-5 (paper)
ISBN 978-0-8077-6415-2 (hardcover)
ISBN 978-0-8077-7869-2 (ebook)

Printed on acid-free paper
Manufactured in the United States of America

With faith in our students, hope for their students, and love for our families—especially Will, Dennis, and Tom—who cheered us on.

Contents

Introduction

Developing Effective Special Educators: Building Bridges Across the Profession has been written to support an educator's journey from teacher preparation to leadership. The purpose of this work is to renew understanding of theory and practice in special education, and to propose that employing epistemic empathy is the best tool for doing so.

There are five major components of this book:

- Examination of how learning theory shapes the argument for the purposeful application of epistemic empathy
- The promise of epistemic empathy
- Instructional principles and strategies
- The story of Ruby and her associates
- The metaphor of the bridge

HOW LEARNING THEORY SHAPES THE ARGUMENT FOR EPISTEMIC EMPATHY

What makes professionals persist and thrive? The discipline of special education is at a crossroads. Although the number of students with disabilities has remained consistent or, in some situations, increased, the number of special educators has declined (Samuels, 2018). As is evident from the high attrition of special educators, knowledge and skills are not enough. If they were, the profession would not be at such a critical juncture. Special educators are needed, but practicing teachers must be licensed, which demands that they possess the relevant knowledge and skills. The field must attract more professionals who will commit to staying, but how do we retain effective special educators? What makes professionals persist and thrive in a field? Research suggests people value their positions when they feel respected and understood, when communication in the workplace is open and honest (Bunting, 2007). The field of special education requires a bridge to build communication and empathy among professionals, their learners, and their leaders. Epistemic empathy, the ability to understand another's thinking and perception, is that bridge. For the field to be vibrant, teachers must persist and grow. Learning theory sheds light on the conditions that promote such resilience and growth.

Constructivism (Matthews, 2003) is theory centered around the notion that learners make new meaning based on their prior knowledge and experiences. They deepen their understanding by adding new information to that which exists. Constructivism drives the teacher preparation model: Preservice teachers learn from professors and materials, and then add to their mental landscape by spending time in the field working with practitioners and students. This field experience, moving from theory to practice, is the nexus between constructivism and Vygotsky's theory of social interaction (Matthews, 2003).

Vygotsky's contribution to learning theory included the notion that, although learning is a personal effort, knowledge is best accrued in social situations where students construct meaning together. Furthermore, Vygotsky offered that the social situations should meet certain criteria: One group member must be "the knowledgeable other," and the learner must be working in the "zone of proximal development."

Vygotsky's explanation of the zone of proximal development (ZPD) is the principle of learning theory that recognizes that novices learn better when they work with those who are closely aligned yet developmentally advanced. Social interaction is valued and practiced; learners and their "knowledgeable others" may construct new knowledge together. When a person is modeling for another, the experience requires that the teacher analyze that which has become automatic so as to better scaffold for the learner; thus, benefits are not only accorded to the learners but to the teachers as well (Baptiste & Sheerer, 1997; Gallucci, 2008; Kuusisaari, 2014; Shabani, 2016; Williams, 2001). According to Gallimore and Tharp (1990), the zone of proximal development, where the learner is led by those with more experience, is not unidirectional. They write, "Assistance and teaching do not flow in one direction. Employees also assist supervisors, pupils teach teachers, teachers assist principals. In any interaction, influences are reciprocal" (p. 189). Reciprocity promotes an environment of trust. All members are contributing toward the goal and are valued. The ZPD is more fluid than fixed. Indeed, all participants may, at one time or another, be the learner or the "knowledgeable other." Reciprocal teaching is beneficial to all.

The combination of epistemic empathy and social interaction is built on constructivist theory, social interaction theory, the zone of proximal development, and the effectiveness of reciprocal learning.

THE PROMISE OF EPISTEMIC EMPATHY

When a student is diagnosed with a disability, perspectives change. Students with disabilities count on their teachers being able to understand different ways of thinking and feeling. The student needs guidance to grapple with the mysteries of learning. Parents are introduced to a unique system of advocacy and understanding. The teacher's attention is focused on meeting individual students' needs while managing the process. Administrators are attentive to the special requirements necessary to ensure that the student receives an appropriate education. *Empathy*, the ability to understand the feelings of others, reduces the tensions these demands inevitably produce. *Epistemic* empathy, the ability to understand the cognitive as well as affective reactions of another, can foster respect for the experiences of the various stakeholders.

Teachers practicing epistemic empathy identify with the reasoning behind students' decisions, parents' requests, and administrators' priorities. By viewing challenges through the perspective of others, teachers can better match instruction to learning. Epistemic empathy has the potential to promote better communication, increased respect, and more learning.

Literature on the importance of empathy in teaching abounds (Cooper, 2004; Lavian, 2013; Sova & Turcan, 2016; Swan & Riley, 2015). Swan and Riley (2015) write that empathy is "generally regarded to be an ability to understand others' emotions, perspectives, or situations and to resonate with or experience the other's emotional state. Such empathy, with the emphasis on affective identification, may be developed through experiences, exercises, and reflective activities" (p. 222). As Bouton (2016) writes, "Understanding the other is essential for teachers, and supporting the development of empathy in novice teachers is important." However, empathy does not only apply to understanding the feelings of others. Steinberg (2014) argues that the epistemic reason for improving empathy is that it trains us to attend to the perspectives of others, and that the demographics of education are changing, and the teacher population is not keeping pace. Building epistemic empathy is vital in this situation.

According to National Center for Education Statistics (NCES), the 2026 projection for new teachers is 354,000 in both public and private schools. These numbers contribute to the projected 3.8 million teachers who will be teaching students in 2026 (Hussar & Bailey, 2018). These teachers demographically are 90% White females who grew up lower-middle or middle class, and in rural or suburban homes (Chou, 2007; Gomez, 1994; Hodgkinson, 2002; Marbley et al., 2007) and who are primarily monolingual (Gomez, 1994). These same teachers will, however, be teaching a growing number of racially, ethnically, and culturally diverse students. According to Hussar and Bailey (2018), the percentage of White students enrolled in elementary and secondary public schools was 64.8% in 1995 and is projected to drop to 45.2% by 2026 (p. 46). Epistemic empathy will allow teachers to reach and teach students with a range of feelings, perspectives, and ways of thinking.

In many ways, epistemic empathy is at the core of special education. By definition, epistemic empathy is the ability to recognize how another person thinks differently. That has been the role of special educators; students with disabilities very often think differently as a direct result of the disability. However, the practice of epistemic empathy can be expanded and has the potential to increase learning for all stakeholders in a learning community. As the diversity of students expands, epistemic empathy will be important for building culturally responsive pedagogy. Improving epistemic empathy among special educators will enhance their understanding of the judgments of others and assist them in developing instruction for learners whose backgrounds do not match their own.

Epistemic empathy also has implications for strengthening the field of special education. Forging social interaction with "knowledgeable others" will allow novices to develop understanding of the decisionmaking processes employed by their leaders. Exercising epistemic empathy will provide a type of leadership training! Epistemic empathy bridges understanding between student and teacher as well as between novice and mentor.

At the end of each chapter, readers of this book are provided with exercises designed to build epistemic empathy. Through these exercises, readers have the opportunity to improve understanding of and collaboration with their students, colleagues, and leaders. Epistemic empathy has the potential to increase teacher effectiveness, allow teachers to bridge demographic differences, and foster teachers' resilience. With each exercise, a bridge builder has been added to structure the conversation and optimize epistemic empathy. The key terms used in the Bridge Builder exercises are building blocks for a problem-solving process that is offered in the final chapters. In the BRIDGE process, problem solving begins by employing epistemic empathy.

INSTRUCTIONAL PRINCIPLES AND PRACTICES

Teachers who practice epistemic empathy will recognize that students who present varied perspectives require varied instructional strategies. These principles and practices will be reviewed in the chapters to follow. In addition to high-leverage practices and performance standards, readers will be provided with information regarding planning, behavior management, specialized curriculum, social and emotional learning, and legal guidelines.

The knowledge and skills needed to be an effective special educator are known. This information is powerful, effective, and useful, and will be reviewed. As novice special educators face increasing demands, it is vital that they have best practices at the ready.

THE STORY OF RUBY AND HER ASSOCIATES

And then there is Ruby. Along the way, the reader will encounter Ruby, a teacher progressing along in her career. As the book begins, she is completing teacher preparation, and is excited to join the profession. She has mastered all that was presented to her as a student and is ready to start. Sure of her knowledge of the laws and guidelines shaping special education, Ruby is confident. She has been planning lessons, designing behavior management systems, and decorating her room. The reader will travel with her through those early days. We expect the outlines of her story to be familiar to our readers; their epistemic empathy will come naturally, as they will know how Ruby feels and thinks about her next big step.

Moving forward, the reader meets Ruby during her first term on the job. Again, the reader will not have to stretch too far to recognize Ruby's joys and frustrations. As she grapples with specialized curricula, a plethora of standards, and the social and emotional needs of her students, Ruby begins to unravel a bit. Rather than employing best practices consistently, the novice teacher becomes reactive. Epistemic Empathy Exercises will allow readers at all stages of their careers to see the storm brewing from varied perspectives.

As Ruby gains wisdom and experience, she is asked to serve as a mentor. Here is the chance to observe Ruby as she employs epistemic empathy with her young colleagues. Confident at this point, she does not hesitate to reach out to others for assistance and support. Epistemic empathy combined with social interaction makes Ruby's mentoring a tour de force! It is instructive to notice that, although her stressors change, she employs what she's learned from those who have shown her the way.

Finally, Ruby reaches a leadership position. Because she has experienced structured interactions with "knowledgeable others," employed epistemic empathy to gain additional perspective, and kept abreast of best practices, Ruby is in good shape to lead the next generation of special educators. She is never perfect; she's not consistently on target, but she is always trying to better the lives of her students. Ruby is one of us.

THE METAPHOR OF THE BRIDGE

Throughout the book, the reader will encounter photos and descriptions of bridges. The symbol of the bridge will be used to emphasize the transitions Ruby makes as she builds her practice, employs epistemic empathy, and depends on social interaction to sustain her professionally. Ruby's move from teacher preparation to her first real job is represented by the Brooklyn Bridge. This iconic bridge is a masterpiece of engineering. It reminds the reader of the importance of a strong foundation. Next, the reader is centered on Ruby's maturing professionalism as represented by the Rolling Bridge. The bridge is able to change shape—curling up or straightening out to meet the requirements of the travelers. It is a symbol reminding the reader of the importance of being flexible in order to meet the needs of the students. The third bridge, the Mostar Bridge, symbolizes the power of collaboration. The very existence of the Mostar Bridge is attributed to collaboration among various countries and agencies. Finally, the Providence Pedestrian Bridge reminds the reader that learning is continuous. The empty space reminds the reader of the power of potential. This pedestrian span is one where folks travel both ways, stop to play a game of chess, or take a moment to appreciate the view. This bridge captures the essence of the book—that knowledge and skills are vital, but that support comes from all directions; we are traveling together, and we mustn't lose sight of where we're going, where we've been, and with whom we are making the journey.

THE BRIDGE SOLUTION

The BRIDGE Solution proposes a process where epistemic empathy is fundamental to problem solving. This serves to guide teachers in applying the principles behind this book as described at the end of the book.

THE BROOKLYN BRIDGE

The Brooklyn Bridge, an American icon, is lauded for its grandeur. Sweeping across the East River, the bridge is a masterpiece of engineering and beauty. However, perhaps its most impressive feature goes largely unnoticed by pedestrians who stroll across the span. In his book *The Great Bridge*, David McCullough quotes the chief engineer, John A. Roebling, as he emphasizes the importance of a solid base: "The foundations for the support of these large masses of masonry must be unyielding" (McCullough, 1972, p. 173). The chapters in Crossing I will describe techniques and principles special educators can use to build a solid base for their teaching. Fortified by knowledge of the law, best practices for planning instruction, and effective behavior management tools, the novice special educator can be confident of a strong foundation. On these points, they, too, must be unyielding.

RUBY BEGINS

The story of Ruby begins here. In her teacher preparation program, Ruby has developed a strong theoretical foundation. She has spent time in a wide variety of classrooms and has completed her student teaching. She possesses foundational knowledge. Now is her time to test that foundation.

At commencement from university, Ruby tossed her hat into the air with the rest of the joyful grads. She hugged and thanked her parents and her clinical supervisor, Ms. Rok, whom she'd invited to the ceremony. As the evening waned, Ruby took one last walk across the lonely campus, littered with confetti and abandoned carnations. She reminisced about the past 4 years, the friends, the adventures, the all-nighters. Each spot on the campus seemed to hold special meaning: the cafe where she'd fallen in love for the first time, the field where she'd twisted her ankle playing soccer, the academic building where she'd attended her education classes.

Her thoughts shifted to the future. Ruby felt confident about what she'd learned in her preservice program, but was it enough? Ruby had blossomed under the guidance of her clinical educator, and when she was offered a position at the school where she'd student taught, Ruby had been ecstatic. Her university supervisor encouraged Ruby to accept the job, but the words the supervisor had chosen haunted Ruby. She had said, "Go for it, Ruby! You're wonderful with the children, and you'll bring a fresh outlook to the faculty. Don't worry; people will help you, and you'll learn as you go. We were all new once upon a time." Ruby had received outstanding grades from the supervisor, but now the message was: You're a beginner again.

With the final campus stroll ended, and her college possessions packed into her old car, Ruby's confidence began to flicker. She was headed home for the summer, perhaps the last summer she'd spend at her parents' house. During the last 4 years Ruby had realized how sheltered her upbringing had been. She'd grown up in a homogeneous environment. She and her friends attended scouts together, belonged to the same teams, went to the same church. Their moms even made similar suppers! Intellectually, she knew her students would have varied backgrounds and experiences. She had read all she could about different cultures, and she'd learned about equity; she believed people to be equal. However, she knew she lacked experience.

Ruby pondered all she'd learned. She could recite guidelines and protocols. Would she be able to follow and fulfil the laws that regulated her teaching practice? She remembered her first Methods class; she'd started off thinking that good instruction centered on engagement without giving much thought to assessing students' gains. Her understanding of that had changed, and she had come to understand that that engagement is important, but not the only part of instruction. Four years ago—it seemed like a lifetime. Ruby had been so excited—and overconfident! She was still excited, but now Ruby was grounded. She knew enough to know she had much to learn. In fact, she was already gathering information about exciting new graduate programs. When she pulled into the driveway of her childhood home, friends and family and cake awaited her. She pushed aside her worries and bounded in to the warm welcome.

She had been scared yet elated when she'd secured a job for the following September several towns away from where she'd grown up. It was her dream job. She'd be providing resource help as well as co-teaching in an inclusion classroom for fourth-graders. Ruby had a passion for teaching children with special needs. She loved to discover their different ways of thinking and learning and design instruction for the ways students learn. The school was in the center of a once thriving community, battered by the latest recession. Many of the students' parents had attended the school in which their children were now enrolled; they had never left the community.

During that summer, Ruby practiced her morning drive to school seven times. She visited all the common areas in the community: supermarket, library, and ice cream shop. She prided herself on her punctuality and wanted to make a good first impression. If she left early enough, she'd have time to check materials and classroom and calm herself down.

Ruby hadn't realized it, but her rehearsal trips occurred during vacation season. By the first day of school, traffic had fallen off significantly. Ruby turned into the parking lot before the folks from maintenance had a chance to unlock the doors. She sat in her car, alone with her thoughts, her excitement, and her anxiety.

A special educator. It's all she'd dreamed of since she'd played school as a child. But during the last four years, she'd discovered how much more there was to the profession. When beginning her teacher preparation program, she'd been impatient to get to the fun! Looking back, she had to admit that the program's early attention to theory and law had grounded her well. She knew she was good at creating engaging lessons. She now knew that those lessons didn't exist in a vacuum; she now knew that data and student need had to drive the development of her lessons. The janitor, unlocking the front door, saw Ruby and motioned her to enter. She gathered up her bags—oh! teachers and their bags—and she strode toward her new life.

Ruby arrived at the door to the classroom and paused to assess the space. She and the general educator had posted "Welcome" signs in English and in the first languages of their five English learners. Suddenly she was unsure. Maybe that wasn't the right way to make her English learners feel welcomed? Her name and that of the co-teacher were posted on the door, and the sight made her heart race. The two teachers had talked about the environment they wanted to create. The general educator had accumulated so many materials during his decade of teaching and could offer many materials for their consideration. They had spent most of August organizing and decorating the room.

Ruby walked into the classroom. There was a name tag for each child and the desks had been arranged in groups of four for increased collaboration. As she reviewed the names, Ruby quietly recited the accommodations and modifications required by IEPs. The teachers had established several stations with Universal Design in mind. Math manipulatives were on a table in front of a whiteboard; books in several languages were in a basket near some comfy pillows, and a rug divided into squares with tape lay in front of the projector. Ruby was alerted by the rumbling of buses. She remade her ponytail, smoothed down the first-day outfit over which she'd fretted all summer, planted her biggest smile on her face, and headed out to greet her children.

Mentor

Ms. Rok, Ruby's former clinical educator, had been honored when the student teacher had invited her to commencement exercises. The ceremony was moving, and it made Ms. Rok wistful. After it ended, Ms. Rok stopped by her classroom to resume packing up for the summer break. It was astonishing how much one could accumulate in 20 years as a special educator. She laughed to herself as she remembered her husband referring to her classroom as an "archaeological dig." It was true; the annual packing allowed her to glimpse her own timeline. She had all sorts of treasures; yearly upgrades to packaged curricula, ever-improving technologies, professional development artifacts that captured the essence of each year's "silver bullet." Ms. Rok was committed to being the teacher her beloved students deserved, so she attended workshops, purchased resources, learned the latest best practices. This year's professional development sessions had focused on special education law, instructional planning, and behavior management. She glanced again at each handout before filing it away, sighing at the weight of a teacher's responsibilities. She'd rest for a few weeks, but then it would be back to work.

Ms. Rok loved to be in the classroom on summer mornings. Her room was filled with fresh air and sunlight, and quiet! The summer months gave her a chance to regroup, reorganize, and plan. One challenge for the year ahead would be her mentorship of Ruby. She had strongly endorsed hiring Ruby, her student teacher. Ruby had great potential, and their work together had been productive. Not every day with Ruby was a resounding success, and the new teacher still had a long way to go, but they, along with Mr. Ford, had developed a good working relationship.

Will Ford championed the value of empathy, particularly encouraging colleagues to imagine the feelings of others before acting. Under his leadership, the faculty and staff were encouraged to consider the experiences of others, to listen to each other carefully and respect each other's points of view. When Ford led the group through a data mining exercise, he began with the directive to watch out for the feelings of others. Ms. Rok believed that congenial experience had helped her boost her students' scores. It had been the best year of her professional life, and she looked forward to continuing their collaboration during the year ahead. But she would have to balance moving forward with helping Ruby get adjusted.

Leader

Will Ford gazed at the raindrops streaming down his windows. A September storm was a thing of beauty, but how the rain played havoc with his knees. Playing sports had been such an important part of his life, but there sure was a price to pay in middle age. Ford checked out the playing fields below. They were very much in need of an overhaul, but then again, so many things were.

Will Ford was gearing up for the opening bell. Today he would begin his third year as principal, a job he'd pursued with passion. Ford wanted to bring all he'd learned on the playing fields and in the classroom to his leadership position. He was determined to lead a school where faculty and students would thrive.

As had been recommended by everyone who preceded him down this road, he'd spent the first 2 years observing and learning. He got to know everyone who worked in his school. He listened to stories, reports, complaints, and praise. That first year was wonderful; the cheers he received reminded him of his days as goalie.

Over the summer, Ford had read up on how deliberate training in empathy helped groups operate better. He decided to experiment with deliberately practicing epistemic empathy—learning to assume the perspective of the other person, as well as to feel their feelings— as an important step in task execution. Ms. Rok and Ruby would be members of the test group; together, they'd learn the process and see how it helped them get through the school year. Ford made sure he, too, was a member of the group.

As you read the chapters in Crossing I, begin to build your epistemic empathy. Consider the chapters' issues from the perspectives of Ruby, Ms. Rok, and Mr. Ford. What questions would each have about these issues? How will special education legislation impact their roles differently? What opportunities and challenges will each find in planning instruction? How is the relationship between their roles and student behavior different? Who works most closely with the students? The parents? The community?

At the conclusion of each chapter, use the Bridge Builder to complete the Epistemic Empathy Exercise, which will post an unstructured problem requiring application of knowledge and skills addressed in the chapter. The exercise will provide an opportunity to think about decisionmaking from varied perspectives.

CHAPTER 1

Special Education Policy

Three major pieces of legislation have shaped the service and delivery of special education. Each has contributed unique specifications, but all have informed the profession. Together, they have improved education for students with disabilities. The current federal law impacting public education, known as ESSA, is entitled Every Student Succeeds Act. The Individuals with Disabilities Act (IDEA) more specifically targets the rights of and responsibilities toward students with special needs. The final piece of legislation, Section 504 of the Rehabilitation Act of 1973, addresses civil rights and protections for persons with disabilities. The field of special education has been impacted profoundly by each of these laws.

REVIEWING ESSA

ESSA is the current nationwide education law for all public schools. The Elementary and Secondary Education Act (ESEA) was first passed in 1965. It has been reauthorized eight times. The latest reauthorization was in December 2015, replacing No Child Left Behind (NCLB) with Every Student Succeeds Act (ESSA). Schools are accountable for how students progress in their learning. Students in special education must be provided with equal opportunity for learning (U.S. Department of Education, 2017; Samuels, 2017).

Implications for students. ESSA specifies that states must provide a quality education for all students, including those in special education. All states submit plans that demonstrate compliance. In every state plan, there are many required components. Six of these points have the most impact on quality special education. *Academic standards* are applied to all students with the goal of preparing them for college and career. *Annual testing* that is required by ESSA specifies that students' IEPs or 504 plans include testing accommodations, so all students can access state testing. Further, only 1% of all students can take alternative assessments, so this will include only a small number of students with significant disabilities. ESSA also requires that states measure school performance—*school accountability*. This is important for students in special education because the goal is for all schools in every state to move all students forward. States set ambitious goals for *academic achievement* for all students, including those who are in special education. Evidence-based teaching benefiting all students is specified in *school improvement plans*. *Report cards* relay subgroup performances including students in special education. This information can then be reviewed to determine if changes in teaching and learning strategies are needed for students in special education.

Implications for teachers. Three components of ESSA impact teachers in special education. First, ESSA has a single requirement for all special education personnel, which is that they obtain full state certification as a special education teacher. This may be through alternative route or state special education testing. (This is a change from the highly qualified teacher requirement in No Child Left Behind.) According to ESSA, individual states must establish their own certification standard. Second, a national center for literacy and reading was created to serve as a clearinghouse with a primary focus on supporting learners who need more help in literacy (Center for Parent Information and Resources, 2018). Third, ESSA focuses on school innovation for supporting all students including those in special education.

REVIEWING IDEA

In 1975 the Federal law for students with disabilities known as the Education for All Handicapped Children Act (PL 94-142) was passed. It was reauthorized and renamed in 1990, becoming the Individuals with Disabilities Education Act (IDEA), and was amended in 2004.

Implications for students. The law guarantees students with disabilities access to public school education. The central feature of the law's implementation is the individualized education plan, or the IEP. Services are available beginning at birth. Transition planning is required for moving into adulthood (Friend, 2018).

Implications for teachers. The six key principles in IDEA provide for the teachers a framework for delivering special education. Teachers, administrators, and related service providers must ensure compliance (Turnbull et al., 2013).

The principle of *zero reject* ensures that all students with disabilities have a right to public education. This includes all disabilities, no matter the severity or nature of the disability. It also includes screenings to ensure that all students with disabilities are identified to receive services (Friend, 2018).

Nondiscriminatory evaluation must be used. This means placement decisions are based on appropriate evaluation. To accomplish this, evaluators must be properly trained to administer assessments and interpret the results. Also, the process and materials must be unbiased. Assessments need to be conducted in the student's native language and be appropriate for the child's characteristics and age. Lastly, multiple assessments must be used to determine the presence of a disability (Yell & Drasgow, 2007).

A *free appropriate public education* (FAPE) is required for all students with a disability. This is accomplished through the design and implementation of the Individualized Education Plan (IEP). The IEP, and Individualized Family Service Plan (IFSP) for children from birth to 3 years, are designed to ensure meaningful education that matches the student (Prince et al., 2018).

Least restrictive environment (LRE) requires that students with an IEP be educated in settings where they can succeed with the needed supports and services. It is presumed that this setting for most students is the general education classroom. Educators must justify when students with an IEP are not in settings with their nondisabled peers (Marx et al., 2014).

Procedural safeguards ensure that any decision made with regard to a student with a disability has parent input and is in compliance with the law (Osborne & Russo, 2014). Parents must give written consent for their children to be assessed to determine a disability, must be invited to meetings, and must give permission for special education to begin. If there is a disagreement between parents and school personnel on any aspects of special education, specific steps must be followed to resolve the dispute.

Finally, IDEA guarantees *participatory rights* to families. These include parents having the right to participate in the special education process and families having the right to confidentiality. This means parents provide input into the design of the IEP (Salend, 2016). Also, information about a student's disability is confidential. Information is to be shared only with individuals working directly with the student. Furthermore, parents have the right to access all records and may dispute information deemed inaccurate (Friend, 2018).

REVIEWING SECTION 504

Section 504 brings the principles of civil rights law to the category of disability (unlike ESSA/IDEA, which govern funding; Salend, 2016).

Implications for students. More students may receive support because Section 504 is based on a broader definition of disabilities. Supports not provided by the education acts (ESSA, IDEA) may be found under this civil rights law. For example, a student with attention deficit disorder may be provided with accommodations of frequent breaks and preferential seating. A student with a health condition such as Type I diabetes, even though an average learner, is able to have access to snacks or juice based on the diagnosed medical condition (Friend, 2018). Section 504 also covers students over 21 or those who have a learning disability not severe enough to meet the IDEA definition (Salend, 2016).

Section 504 also addresses access to nonacademic and extracurricular activities. This means that fieldtrips and after-school programs need to be accessible to all students. Access doesn't always mean participation. For example, all students have the right to try out for a team and selection can still be based on required skills (Salend, 2016).

Implications for teachers. Teachers can see the similarities between Section 504 and IDEA. Students who qualify under Section 504 *or* IDEA have a right to an appropriate education (FAPE) and these students are all educated with nondisabled peers to the maximum extent possible (LRE). Nondiscriminatory evaluation and team decisionmaking are required by teachers in both Section 504 and IDEA. Lastly, due process where families have the right to an impartial hearing and to be represented by counsel are supported in both (Bartlett et al., 2007; Shaw & Madaus, 2008).

IMPLEMENTING THE LEGISLATION

Each piece of legislation has established specific requirements regarding implementation and accountability.

IEP and IFSP. IDEA requires a written Individualized Education Plan (IEP) to guide the student's education between the ages of 3 and 21. All IEPs must include the following components: general student and family information, present levels of performance—academic and functional, annual goals/benchmarks/objectives, services, and supplementary aids including assistive technology. Notice as to how and when the goals/objectives/benchmarks will be measured is required. In an IEP there are two sections about goals/objectives/benchmarks. One section addresses how they will be monitored and the other when they will be monitored. Rationale when the student is not participating with nondisabled peers must be given. Dates for the IEP and signatures from all participants must be included. Students must be invited to participate in their own IEP at the age of 14 and transition planning is required no later than age 16. Lastly, information from the student and family should be incorporated into the IEP (Friend, 2018). For children from birth to age 3, a comparable document is required. The Individualized Family Service Plan (IFSP) is developed for children birth through age 2 by a team including the family. Some states extend the IFSP through age 3 or age 5. The components in an IFSP include: present level of development; assessment of family's strengths, needs, priorities, concerns for enhancing the child's needs; outcomes; assessments; early education, natural environment for services; dates; coordinator; procedure for moving from early intervention to preschool; and annual evaluation (Salend, 2016).

Section 504 plan. This accommodation plan typically includes statements of the nature and impact of disability, student's strengths and challenges, and accommodations and supports. Follow-up dates and persons responsible for accommodations are also part of the plan (Salend, 2016).

Successful implementation of any of the plans will be fostered by communicating meaningful information to all parties about the plans (Goodman et al., 2011; Yell et al., 2013). For example, service hours as specified in the plans should be clear to those providing services. Discussion about transition plans, whether in the IEP or IFSP, is also necessary among all parties.

EPISTEMIC EMPATHY EXERCISE

Ruby's days were fraught. She always seemed a step or two behind; either she couldn't get to every student before the bell rang or the paperwork wasn't done. There were so many responsibilities, and she just couldn't manage. Ruby was grateful for any help she could get, so when her fourth-grade counterpart gave her some advice, Ruby clutched it as if it were a life preserver.

Just the week before, Ruby had attended an IEP meeting for Dennis, a student with a language processing problem. Because her confidence was waning, Ruby had deferred to others in the room, and as a result, she felt the resulting IEP could have been more explicit. She'd just have to double down and give more attention to Dennis, especially since the speech therapy designated in the IEP was not forthcoming. Apparently, the district could not afford a full-time speech therapist. Ruby had been surprised by that; she'd expected the district to comply.

When she complained in the teachers' room about the lack of speech therapy, Judy, the fourth-grade teacher, said, "That's easy to fix. Just call the parents and tell them that the IEP requirements aren't being met!" And that's just what Ruby did, thinking to herself that such a phone call would result in one less problem.

She was wrong about that, which was how she landed in Mr. Ford's office on Friday afternoon, accompanied by her mentor, Ms. Rok, and the union representative. Ruby had made the wrong call. What do you think happened next?

BRIDGE BUILDER

The graphic organizer below will help you structure your discussion of the issue presented in the Epistemic Empathy Exercise. In the left column are listed the persons involved in the dilemma. Respond to the questions in the right column as the designated person would respond. Use epistemic empathy; take the perspective of another in order to analyze the issue. Collaborate to solve the problem.

Ruby	How did Mr. Ford feel when he discovered I called the parent? How did Ms. Rok feel when she had to represent me and I did not confide in her about my problem?
Mr. Ford	Why would Ruby call a parent without speaking to Ms. Rok or myself? How does Ms. Rok feel about being left out of the conversation?
Ms. Rok	Why didn't Ruby come to me with her concerns? How did Mr. Ford feel when he received the information about Ruby calling the parent and complaining about lack of services?
Collaborative Solution	How can we *build* a team solution to satisfy both the parents and the administration? What can we do as a team to *build* our communication so that this problem will not happen again?

CHAPTER 2

Instructional Planning

Planning instruction for all students is an intricate process. Theory and practice are uniquely integrated at the point of planning. An effective teacher links new knowledge to that which the student already owns; objectives and assessment must be closely linked, and engagement designed to ensure student participation. In addition, a lesson is better targeted when it is based on data. Curriculum-based measures, standardized test scores, and observational data give the teacher information for how and where to situate a lesson so that it is most impactful for students. When planning for students with disabilities, the teacher will also be guided by the students' IEPs. Choosing from among myriad strategies and resources is a difficult process made easier when shaped by the use of data.

GATHERING DATA

Data from a variety of sources helps the special educator get to know the child's interests, abilities, and challenges. The goal of the educator is to develop a learner profile for each student (Brownell, 2019). An example of a rich profile is one that includes information well beyond a sheet of test scores; it may incorporate the student's cultural and linguistic experiences, co-curricular activities, and work samples. This treasure trove of information should be shared among all professionals working with the student, each of whom will provide unique insights.

Based on the analysis of the profile, the team determines the instructional interventions that show most promise for the spotlighted child. Special educators implement these interventions, maintaining data as the child progresses. This is the essence of the data cycle. The student is pre-assessed on his or her knowledge of the curriculum. The curriculum is assessed for appropriateness for the student. As instruction takes place, the student is informally and formally assessed, providing further data. Once the lesson has been completed, all data—observational, work samples, and test scores—are gathered and assessed so as to inform further instruction. Student learning must be designed based on data; student learning must be monitored using feedback data, and new instruction designed using new data.

Data is to be used for all educational decisions. For students with disabilities, evidence of student response is useful for making decisions regarding next steps. Teachers make decisions about instruction to be selected, duration of intervention, and the intensity of the work (Glover & Vaughn, 2010; Vaughn & Bos, 2015).

Suggestions for Data-Based Instruction

- Keep data collections simple and consistent.
- Use progress monitoring to understand if intervention is working.
- Remember that groups can be reconfigured to meet student needs.
- Be flexible. If instruction is not working, make a change.
- Develop an easy, reliable method for recording.

INCORPORATING BEST PRACTICE

Analysis of data shapes planning of instruction. Teachers then choose from well-vetted practices to match the lesson to student need. Two such practices are Universal Design for Learning (UDL) and Differentiated Instruction (DI).

UDL. Universal Design for Learning is a collection of principles that, when applied to learning environments, increases accessibility for all learners (Nelson, 2014). The principles of UDL guide the teacher toward recognizing and minimizing barriers to accessing the curriculum. UDL is proactive; therefore, it is not targeted at the special needs of a single student. Rather, it suggests the teacher acknowledges all barriers and removes as many as possible, allowing access to a wide variety of students. When the special educator collaborates with the general educator to design a lesson with an accommodation for a student with a disability, other students may benefit. For example, a student with a disability may require a visual checklist of the steps in the lesson; however, many students will find this visual checklist helpful, too. Therefore, in an inclusion classroom everyone may benefit from the wide variety of options that UDL provides.

UDL requires teachers to offer multiple means of engagement, representation, and expression. *Engagement* means making sure topics are of interest to students. Letting students choose a book to read or a topic for research, or using student names in math problems, are examples of engagement. *Representation* refers to the medium through which a student is delivered new information. For representation, teachers often offer videos as well as textbooks when teaching a new concept. This is very helpful to a student who has comprehension issues. Some students are very knowledgeable about a topic but have difficulty getting words onto paper and find it helpful to utilize speech-to-text software. This is an example of a means of *expression*.

Suggestions for Incorporating UDL

- Use closed captioning when watching a video.
- Allow students to listen to an audio version or read a text.
- Provide flexible seating options, including allowing students to choose seating.
- Include digital options such as creating a podcast instead of writing a paper.

DI. Differentiated Instruction is fundamental to special education. It is based on the premise that students learn differently and require varied materials, forms of instruction, and means of assessment. Teachers who differentiate instruction know their students, know how they learn, and know what motivates them. Teachers who differentiate set the stage for all learners to work hard and to achieve more (Tomlinson, 2014).

Educators employing DI differentiate the content, process, or product of a learning experience. By differentiating the *content*, teachers offer their students a variety of ways to gain access to the content. Differentiating by *process* provides students more than one way to make sense of a concept. This lends itself to supporting students with disabilities who often need repetition and a multisensory approach (Tomlinson, 2001). Teachers can differentiate the *product* by giving students a menu of items to be completed to demonstrate what they have learned. Students find this choice empowering and will typically produce better work due to increased engagement (Tomlinson, 2014). If students are being taught in a way that meets their own needs, including students with disabilities becomes organic.

Teachers can also differentiate by learning style, readiness, and interest (Tomlinson, 2014). Differentiating by *learning style* provides students an opportunity to absorb and engage with new information in the manner that is best for them. *Readiness* is the most common way to differentiate. Students are often grouped by similar skills and work in small homogeneous groups particularly in reading and math. Differentiating by *interest* can be as simple as allowing students to choose what book to read or what topic to research.

Suggestions for Incorporating DI

- Offer topic or content choice to students. Students feel empowered when given a choice of topics and will be more motivated to complete the task.
- Make available multimodal materials—such as online materials, hands-on models, and hard copies of materials. Also provide a variety of supports such as graphic organizers, multiplication tables, and word banks.
- Use learning stations to allow students to work in small groups and to give the teacher time to work individually with students.
- Assign differentiated homework. This will avoid frustration at home. Students will have homework that they are able to complete independently.

CONSIDERING ADDITIONAL STRATEGIES

Special educators will be skilled at using peer-reviewed practices in teaching. The Council for Exceptional Children & CEEDAR Center have created a guide for such practices, which they call high-leverage practices (HLPs) in special education (Council for Exceptional Children & CEEDAR Center, 2017). These 22 HLPs address collaboration, assessment, social/emotional/behavioral practices and instruction. Instruction HLPs are considered below.

Goal setting. Special educators need to be able to move students forward in their learning goals. Appropriate goals are identified and prioritized as long- or short-term. The goals are determined based on standards, the IEP, and the curriculum. Teachers determine what must be accomplished now and what can wait for later (Alber-Morgan, Konrad et al., 2019). Once goals are established and prioritized, special educators systematically design the instruction to reach these goals. They determine the depth, breadth, and sequence of teaching (Konrad et al., 2019). Also, special educators adapt curriculum for student access (Alber-Morgan, Helton et al., 2019).

Strategy instruction. Special educators instruct students in the use of learning strategies to help them learn and perform (Hughes, 2011). Examples include notetaking, time management, reading strategies, and presentation skills.

Scaffolding. Special educators determine the kind of support a student needs. Duration, intensity, planned withdrawal of support are elements of scaffolding (Mariage et al., 2019).

Explicit instruction. Special educators provide a direct approach to provide the student with clarity, guidance, and sufficient support to achieve the outcomes of the lesson (Hughes et al., 2019). Knowledge is transferred and targeted practice is planned.

Flexible groupings. Special educators differentiate instruction and meet students' needs by using different grouping patterns (Maheady et al., 2019). These groupings may consist of students with the same or mixed abilities, and range from individuals, to pairs, to small groups, or whole class (Hoffman, 2002).

There are additional skills a special educator will develop to be effective in reaching and teaching students in special education. Students should be active, involved learners. Heward (2019) discusses decades of research that shows that active student engagement leads to academic achievement and lowers off-task and disruptive behaviors. Special educators use assistive and instructional technologies to address their students' unique needs (Alper & Raharinirina, 2006).

Choosing a strategy is just the beginning. Special educators monitor the strategy's effectiveness through intensive instruction. Intensive instruction requires the use of data-based individualization (DBI) that dictates changes in interventions based on student response to instruction (National Center on Intensive Intervention, 2013). DBI is built on the foundation of effective and immediate feedback. Alberto and Troutman (2013) note that without teaching students to maintain and generalize new knowledge and behaviors, the learning is meaningless. Feedback is best when it clearly informs the students how they are doing in relation to the goal and what can be done to improve progress toward the goal (Doabler et al., 2016; Hattie, 2008). Knowing how to give meaningful, positive, and constructive feedback is an important skill. Such feedback guides students in their learning and leads to students becoming more engaged, more motivated, and ultimately more independent (Council for Exceptional Children & CEEDAR, 2017).

MANAGING DIFFERENT LEVELS OF NEED

Some students are challenged by how they are being taught. Their needs may be met through accommodations. Others find what they are being taught to pose difficulty. Their needs are met through modifications. In the classroom, *accommodations* are the input or output processes that are adjusted in the teaching and learning process, whereas *modifications* are the changes in standards or content (Polloway et al., 2003).

Accommodations are required by many entities. IDEA, Section 504 of the Federal Rehabilitation Act of 1973, and the Americans with Disabilities Act specify the need for accommodations for individuals with disabilities. For example, accommodations might be necessary for an individual to access school curriculum or to enter school or work buildings. Testing accommodations must be included in the IEP (Byrnes, 2000).

Many general accommodations might be considered for a student's IEP, but they must be tailored to the individual needs of the student. Accommodations change how a student learns, not what he learns. Accommodations may include a change in instructional materials such as highlighters, manipulatives, graphic organizers, or calculators. During instruction, accommodations, such as prompts or models, may be provided. Accommodations may be in the form of supplemental materials such as visual schedules or timers, which can help students with transitions. Preferential seating or study carrels might be a useful environmental accommodation (Gargiulo & Metcalf, 2010). This provides a meaningful starting point as a novice special educator determines how to operationalize accommodations for a particular student in a particular setting.

Testing accommodations are often required by students' IEPs. For example, directions might be read aloud, simplified, or repeated.

Students might use extra space on a page, lined paper, or voice recognition technology to aid in test responses. Timing and scheduling testing accommodations may include extended time, breaks during testing, or scheduling testing over multiple days. The testing setting could be individual or small group; study carrels or preferential seating might be specified.

Linguistically based accommodations such as familiar language, translating tests, and pairing visuals with directions are also possible testing accommodations (Salend, 2016). The novice special educator might also consider how some of these accommodations developed for testing could be useful for all students.

Modifications differ from accommodations. Whereas accommodations adjust how a student learns, modifications adjust what a student learns. Some students with disabilities will need modifications for learning. Instructional modifications are generally either reducing what is learned or presenting different content (Gargiulo & Metcalf, 2010; Nolet & McLaughlin, 2005). Modified curriculum often revolves around the same standards or content themes. However, the objectives are changed to match what the student needs.

It is important for the novice special educator to remember that instructional modifications are only for those students with the most significant disabilities, because these modifications reduce the student's opportunity to learn the range of knowledge and skills in a given subject (Friend & Bursuck, 2019). The decision to make modifications is made by the IEP team for students who have such significant disabilities that a change in curricular expectations is warranted. Modifications thus may be different content within a curriculum, like different spelling words or different expectations for homework, or a different curriculum altogether.

Suggestions for Accommodations and Modifications

Accommodations

- Books on tape
- Digital access
- Flexible seating
- Graphic organizers
- Extended time/frequent breaks

Modifications

- Different spelling words
- Leveled textbook
- Reduced assignment
- Different homework

EPISTEMIC EMPATHY EXERCISE

November 10 was Observation Day! Ruby couldn't wait to show off a bit for her mentor teacher, Ms. Rok. Ms. Rok was a sweetheart, but she was old school. Ruby often had to assist her with instructional and assistive technology, and Ms. Rok was always complimenting Ruby's use of the latest materials. At 9:00 a.m., Ms. Rok settled into the last seat in the first row, smiled brightly at Ruby, and dated the top of her notepad.

Ruby's plan went beautifully. She started with a clip from YouTube which explained, in cartoon format, how to recognize a story's main idea. The students loved it and applauded when it was over. Next, she instructed students to type in a URL so that they'd arrive at a specific graphic organizer. She then played a reading of Shirley Jackson's "The Lottery" (1948). The story was short and powerful, and Ruby thought it would work perfectly for students to try out a graphic organizer and identify the main idea.

When the story was over, Ruby directed her students to move into groups with those nearest them. She was confident that randomly grouping students would guarantee them the opportunity to help each other. She asked each group to submit one completed graphic organizer. When they were finished, each group would work together on developing a skit of the short story. Ruby was delighted with the lesson—it had something for everyone.

As the end of the class neared, students asked Ruby for an extension so that they could work on improving their skits. They were excited and cheerful as they headed for the exits, and Ruby was over the moon. She sat down next to Ms. Rok anticipating congratulations. Ruby was shocked when Ms. Rok said quite seriously, "Ruby, we have some serious problems here, and I think we need to meet with Ford." What do you think happened next?

BRIDGE BUILDER

The graphic organizer below will help you structure your discussion of the issue presented in the Epistemic Empathy Exercise. In the left column are listed the persons involved in the dilemma. Respond to the questions in the right column as the designated person would respond. Use epistemic empathy; take the perspective of another in order to analyze the issue. Collaborate to solve the problem.

Ruby	Why was Ms. Rok concerned about this lesson?
	What will Mr. Ford say when we meet?
Mr. Ford	Why is Ms. Rok pulling me into this meeting?
	What did Ruby do in her lesson that caused Ms. Rok to be so concerned?
Ms. Rok	Why was Ruby so surprised when I told her my concerns?
	What will Mr. Ford think of my supervising skills?
Collaborative Solution	How can we *review* the problem as a team and design a solution to satisfy all members of the team?
	What can we do as a team to *build* on our new teacher's previous experience and knowledge and help them to succeed?

CHAPTER 3

Student Behavior

New teachers and veterans alike know that good classroom management establishes the foundation for good learning. Classroom and behavior management are achieved through a teacher's demeanor, skill, and planning. Students may be primed for success by the environment of a classroom, which becomes apparent immediately. A student may sense it simply by the physical arrangement of the room. A student-centered classroom will have the support of the school's program for positive behavior intervention (described below) and will translate that system to support the teacher's ethic. Within the classroom, the effective teacher will establish norms to achieve a positive atmosphere. The goal is to help students internalize their own behavior management. Finally, some students with special needs may need additional, individualized plans to assess, achieve, and maintain productive and positive behavior. All levels of classroom and behavior management require consideration.

PROVIDING AN ENVIRONMENT FOR SUCCESS

Physical environment. Every new teacher has dreamed about setting up a classroom. New teachers spend many hours looking at model classrooms online and can't wait until they have their own. Most teachers spend the month of August setting up the room, but sometimes, when students arrive and occupy the space, it becomes clear that the plan is flawed. Supportive classrooms are designed to meet students' needs.

"Designing learning spaces that meet the needs of our students can be a high-leverage classroom management strategy, especially if the students themselves are involved in some of the decision making" (Dillon, 2018, p. 40). Getting students involved in room design can be powerful. This truly gives them ownership of the room. When the walls frame student work, students know it is valued. Flexible seating is another way to give student ownership in the classroom. When students choose where they want to work, they are more motivated and productive (Dillon, 2018; Kennedy, 2017).

Classrooms that have little clutter, where the teacher has been intentional about displays, allow students to focus longer than fussier ones, and students reported less intellectual exhaustion (Fisher et al., 2014). Intentional use of decorations and color palette matters. Lighting must also be intentional. Most students respond best to natural light; therefore, windows are best when free of clutter. Classroom decorations and lighting are small but powerful elements that can affect classroom environment and student behavior.

Suggestions for Classroom Design

- Curate. Often too much material can be distracting to students.
- Maintain order. Label items so students can put things back where they belong.
- Ensure wide spaces so all students can access all materials.
- Establish spaces for collaboration as well as for individual work.
- Elicit feedback to get the students' perspectives regarding the space.

Emotional environment. Mutual respect is foundational to a supportive learning environment. Mutual respect is demonstrated by the novice special educator having interactions that are welcoming, nonjudgmental, respectful, culturally sensitive, empathetic, and trusting. Students know when their teachers care about them (Ellerbrock et al., 2015). Therefore, establishing this relationship is paramount. Mutual respect is also demonstrated through having high, achievable standards for all students (Henderson, 2013).

The special educator can focus on setting the stage for success for students with disabilities by creating a supportive learning environment. In the beginning of the school year classroom expectations such as consistent routines and procedures are established. When class routines, procedures, and rules are developed, all students should be actively involved in the process. Students with disabilities need to be part of these classroom communities so they, too, have the opportunity to participate in the development (Evertson & Emmer, 2017).

Other students may contribute to creating a positive environment. For example, some students are transient, moving to new school settings or transitioning into different settings throughout the year. A veteran student may serve as the guide and mentor to a student who is new to the setting (Vaughn & Bos, 2015). This support provides an opportunity for the new student to be successful.

Special educators will strive to keep the classroom climate positive throughout the school year. Continuous rotation of displayed student work is one example. Also, knowing students' current interests can provide conversation connections for teacher to student. Attending school and community events shows students that the teacher is part of their world outside the classroom. Class meetings provide opportunities for ongoing dialogue throughout the year. Helping students develop lifelong skills through ongoing constructive feedback supports a positive classroom climate. Teachers who model that failure is part of learning show that the classroom is a safe space to try. Finally, effective special educators maintain a positive perspective when managing student behaviors (Evertson & Emmer, 2017).

Suggestions for Creating a Positive Classroom Environment

- Create three or four classroom rules with the students. Role-play and review the rules frequently.
- Engage in community building activities such as Morning Meeting. (ResponsiveClassroom.org is a great resource for activities.)
- Engage in "getting to know you" activities. Students need to find commonalities with other students to begin to develop a classroom community.
- Share information about yourself. Students need to get to know you just like you want to get to know them.
- Save extra name tags and folders. When a new student comes in during the year, he or she will have the same supplies as the rest of the class.

APPLYING POSITIVE BEHAVIOR INTERVENTION SUPPORTS IN THE CLASSROOM

School-wide PBIS. Positive Behavioral Interventions and Supports (PBIS) is a framework being used for all students (National Education Association, 2014). PBIS was added to IDEA in 1997, and it is the only legislated approach for addressing behavior. Its focus is on using functional assessment and positive methods to promote appropriate behavior. PBIS over the years has been proven effective for developing a positive school community (Horner et al., 2010). PBIS strategies focus on preventing behavior problems by teaching appropriate behaviors (Janney & Snell, 2000).

Sometimes called Schoolwide Positive Behavior Support (SWPBS), the strategy has the goal of keeping schools and classrooms well-managed and safe (Polloway et al., 2018). Common language and expectations throughout the school are a fundamental aspect of SWPBS. Behavior expectations are posted and taught in all locations in the school building, including the lunchroom and hallways. Key practices of SWPBS have been presented by Sprague and Walker (2005). These include the following:

- Expected behaviors are clear and known to students and staff.
- Problem behaviors and consequences are clearly defined.
- Instruction and assistance to move students toward positive social behaviors is ongoing.
- Motivational incentives are used to engage positive behaviors.
- Staff are committed to ongoing implementation of the process; staff receive training, and common language is used throughout the school.

PBIS in the classroom. Classroom teachers are required to convey to the students the schoolwide norms. In addition, it is their role to teach and practice the desired behaviors. Discussions and role-play can be used to identify what "Be respectful" (for example) looks and sounds like in the classroom as well as the playground. PBIS has three tiers of support. The teacher is responsible for implementing and teaching the expectations for most students (tier 1). Some students will require extra support, which may be given by the school counselor (tiers 2 and 3). School counselors will often offer socials skills groups or lunch groups to assist students who are struggling with behaviors.

Students with disabilities are supported in this system. Students are less likely to learn if they do not feel safe, respected, and valued (Ellerbrock et al., 2015). School should be a place where students want to be rather than have to be (Tschannen-Moran & Clement, 2018).

Several challenges may exist when implementing PBIS. Schoolwide rules may differ from classroom rules. It is imperative that students understand the differences. And, on a final note, positive incentives are often given for students who are demonstrating appropriate behavior outside of the classroom. Consideration must be given to the balance of incentives with the guidelines that exist in individual classroom behavior management systems.

IMPLEMENTING A BEHAVIOR INTERVENTION PLAN

Achieving PBIS goals is a challenge for some students with disabilities. More structure than is provided through PBIS may be necessary. When this occurs, a student will need a *behavior intervention plan.*

The process of developing and implementing a behavior intervention plan begins with conducting a functional behavior assessment (FBA). The purpose of such an assessment is to clarify how the student is using behavior to affect change or achieve desired outcomes. In essence, the teacher asks, "What is causing this student to behave in this way?" Once a determination is made about the cause of the behavior, an intervention can be designed (Gresham, 2004). Conducting an FBA involves the following steps: describing the behaviors in observable terms and prioritizing them; describing the settings where the behavior occurs; gathering information using multiple sources, such as interviews, observations, and rating scales; analyzing data; and then developing a hypothesis about the function of the behavior (O'Neill et al., 2015).

Data are reviewed to analyze the antecedents and consequences surrounding the behavior in question. Antecedents are the conditions preceding the student's behavior, and the consequences are the events that occur after the student's behavior (Hirsch et al., 2017). Data are used to reveal patterns. Once a pattern is unveiled, the reason for the behavior is more likely to be evident. Knowing why the behavior is happening allows for effecting a change in the behavior.

The completed FBA is reviewed by the behavior support team (BST) and is the basis for the behavior intervention plan (BIP) they develop. The goal of the BIP is to change a student's behavior by addressing the function of the behavior through a set of well-chosen strategies (Liaupsin, 2015). The BST will determine how to provide the student with a replacement behavior that serves the same function but is socially appropriate, adjust the environment to cue the new behavior, and provide reinforcement that is given at the correct rate and is adequate to support the replacement behavior. BIPs should include antecedent strategies to prevent the inappropriate behavior, strategies to teach the new replacement behavior, and a system to monitor and evaluate implementation of the BIP (Hirsch et al., 2017).

Suggestions for Implementation of BIP

- Inform everyone who works with the student of the behavior plan.
- Communicate with the student's family and encourage reinforcement of the plan outside of school.
- Be consistent in the implementation of the plan.
- Collect data to evaluate the plan's effectiveness.
- Change the plan if the data so indicates.

MAKING STUDENTS ACCOUNTABLE FOR THEIR OWN BEHAVIOR

Every educator's goal is to have students become independent. Some students will need behavior plans for their school careers, but many students will learn the self-regulation skills needed to be successful. To keep the latter students on track, special educators monitor behavior and give consistent, constructive, and positive feedback.

According to Jones et al. (2016), high-quality relationships with students are the best foundation to prevent challenging behavior. In order to cultivate relationships, teachers should validate students' emotions and make students feel secure. One way to do this is to give specific positive feedback when students are behaving appropriately. Students need to know what correct behavior is and to be acknowledged when they exhibit the corrected behavior.

Special educators with a positive mindset do not respond to challenging behavior punitively. To them, challenging behavior is a chance to grow and learn. When students do misbehave, the teacher with a positive approach will ask the student to reflect on the behavior and will discuss what the student can do to change the behavior in the future. Logical consequences are used to help students understand the effect of their behavior on others. For example, if a student writes on the desk, a logical consequence would be to clean the desk. Logical consequences are meaningful responses to misbehavior.

Suggestions for Promoting Student Accountability

- Be sure students understand expectations.
- Have a cool-down area for self-reflection.
- Notice positive behavior and give specific feedback.

- Label misbehavior as a learning opportunity.
- Use logical consequences as opposed to punishment.

EPISTEMIC EMPATHY EXERCISE

As the wildflowers began to bloom, and spring made its grand entrance, Ruby was feeling optimistic. She'd survived the difficulties of late fall, and the legendary reentry after holiday break. Ruby had data to show that her students were making progress toward the benchmarks of their IEPs. She had established a classroom environment where respect was expected and reciprocated. She'd even learned how to chat comfortably in the teachers' lounge, sharing her ideas, but thinking before speaking. As she gained Mr. Ford's confidence, he'd begun to ask her to participate a bit more in school, become more visible at co-curricular events, and she'd been happy to do so. On this day, she'd been assigned lunch duty.

The students filed in, chatting away, some carrying lunchboxes, others headed for the cafeteria food line. Lunchtime was important for students. They could relax a bit, recharge, redirect their energies.

By this time, Ruby was a known entity, and the students were comfortable with her. Some greeted her directly and others waved, though some were so engrossed in their own conversations that they might not have seen her. But on this day, one seventh-grader, Erin, was itching for a fight.

Erin was on Ruby's caseload. She had been diagnosed with emotional/behavior disorder, exacerbated by a volatile family situation. Erin's father had been removed from the home the previous night, and Erin was furious with her mother for allowing it to happen. So when Ruby directed Erin to pick up some trash she'd flung to the ground, Erin lashed out. "You're not my mother!" she screamed. Rather than employing strategies she knew would work with Erin, Ruby reacted emotionally; she said (loudly) to Erin, "No one talks to me that way. Leave this cafeteria at once!" to which Erin responded, "No!" Suddenly there was silence all around. All students were riveted to the showdown. At that very moment, Mr. Ford and Ms. Rok strolled into the cafeteria. What do you think happened next?

BRIDGE BUILDER

The graphic organizer below will help you structure your discussion of the issue presented in the Epistemic Empathy Exercise. In the left column are listed the persons involved in the dilemma. Respond to the questions in the right column as the designated person would respond. Use epistemic empathy; take the perspective of another in order to analyze the issue. Collaborate to solve the problem.

Ruby	What did Ms. Rok think when she walked into the cafeteria and heard me screaming?
	Will this episode change Mr. Ford's impression of me?
Mr. Ford	Why is Ruby screaming in the cafeteria at a student with an emotional behavioral disorder?
	What can Ms. Rok do to help Ruby maintain her self-control when a student bristles her?
Ms. Rok	Why did Ruby lose her self-control?
	What will Mr. Ford think of Ruby after witnessing this behavior?
Collaborative Solution	How can we *review* procedures to support teachers when they are feeling frustrated by student behavior?
	How can we *investigate* strategies as a team and give Ruby some suggestions on how to react when a student has an emotional outburst?

THE ROLLING BRIDGE

The Rolling Bridge designed by Thomas Heatherwick is a high-tech modern drawbridge. Located on Paddington Basin in London, the Rolling Bridge is a beloved tourist attraction. Observers delight at the capability of the bridge to curl up to create open space or unfold to provide access between two points and span to support travelers. It is a metaphor for the talents of special educators. Like the Rolling Bridge, special educators must learn to change to accommodate need. Students' needs vary. Culturally and linguistically diverse students require special outreach. All students, but particularly those challenged by disabilities, need strong social and emotional skills. Curriculum and assessment for students with special needs may need refinement and revision. While the Brooklyn Bridge models the power of strong foundations, the Rolling Bridge bears witness to the importance of flexibility.

RUBY PERSISTS

As Ruby's story continues, the idealistic newbie begins to encounter the more challenging aspects of teaching. Although her confidence wavers, she focuses on deepening her practice. Ruby intensifies her understanding of curriculum and assessment as they relate to her students. Her enhancement of culturally responsive pedagogy and her attention to social-emotional learning improve the educational experience for the students she loves.

Ruby would think back to her first day often as the months passed. It had seemed so orderly then! Intellectually, she knew there would be challenges as there had been when she student-taught, but in her heart, she believed she'd preempted them by memorizing the curriculum. She hoped so, anyway. Pivoting wasn't her strength. Ruby's plans were meticulous. Each day was scheduled in 20-minute intervals.

But by November, Ruby was addressing issues moment to moment. She pictured herself, now, as a juggler with too many balls in the air. Ruby felt such anxiety trying to meet the needs of each student. The language demands of her English learner students with IEPs were confusing, even to her. How would she manage supporting her students through the challenging curriculum? Her only consolation was that she was keeping a close eye on IEPs and making accommodations. However, she wasn't sure they were working. She became reliant on a small list of accommodations, and students were not making adequate progress. Students were shutting down and acting out. The students with IEPs seemed to be feeling isolated from the general population. Worse, they were disrupting cooperative learning groups. She'd intended to provide students from her caseload with opportunities for social and emotional learning, but she just couldn't seem to wedge it into the day.

The teaching assistant had offered repeatedly to help with the more time-consuming logistical problems, but Ruby couldn't bear to reveal to a woman twice her age how disorganized it had all become. Ruby's lowest moment came in late November when she realized she was screaming at her students, hoping they'd grasp meaning from volume. On that day, Ruby cried all the way home. She had wanted to be a great teacher. She had imagined herself boosting learning in and out of school, connecting with diverse families across the community, making school a safe and happy place. Instead, she was playing catch-up, and she felt like a failure.

The memory of raising her voice to her children kept Ruby tossing and turning the entire night. As she readied to return to her class the next morning, Ruby looked into the mirror to give herself a pep talk. "You know this stuff!" she sternly spoke to her own image. "Refresh yourself; put what you learned into practice!" And with a deep breath, the novice headed back to school. She began by reviewing the curriculum, culturally responsive pedagogy, and social–emotional learning.

Mentor

"Uh-oh," thought Ms. Rok when she heard the shouting from the room next door that November day. "Our friend Ruby is beginning to unravel," she said to herself. Ms. Rok felt for the novice teacher. She relived a December day back in 1980-something, driving her VW Bug through a vicious rainstorm, and crying because her observation had gone so badly. "The first year will be the hardest," the principal had kindly said. Ms. Rok wasn't at all sure the principal for whom she and Ruby worked would be as compassionate; he could be caustic.

Ms. Rok had been delighted to be assigned as mentor teacher to Ruby. They'd worked so well in the clinical dyad. She knew Ruby's strengths but was also aware of the young teacher's tendency to yell when she got panicky. Ms. Rok had chosen to wait for Ruby to ask for help, but that approach wasn't working. She texted Ruby, inviting her out for a cup of tea after school. They'd discussed many of the first-year challenges in the previous months, but now it was time to develop some concrete plans. Ms. Rok cringed a bit as she wondered if her own laid-back attitude had left Ruby feeling unsupported.

"Talk to me, Ruby," the older woman said to the younger, as they gazed out the shop window at the sun setting over the bridge. And Ruby spilled her sorrow. She shared that she'd imagined the joy of changing lives, that she'd pictured herself as calm, organized and fun. Ruby understood the theories behind individualization, and the importance of social–emotional learning. As she'd prepared for her job, she imagined herself serving students with poise and grace. Between sobs, Ruby described all the reasons her plans had gone awry: student absenteeism, behavior management missteps, and difficulty with parents. She knew supports existed, but she'd been too embarrassed to ask. Ruby felt she'd failed her students because being calm, organized and fun wasn't sufficient. "And the curriculum!" she wailed. "I've tried to use such great technology to interest the kids, but they just stare at me! I wanted to creatively probe their thinking: instead, I'm spoon-feeding content to my kids. I'm reading directions to students who can't understand them, don't want to do the work, and I sound like a robot when all I wanted was to be a special educator!"

Ms. Rok waited, listening intently for Ruby to question herself rather than assign blame to circumstances, students, or support. The mentor gently placed her hand on her colleague's shoulder.

"I know how you're feeling and thinking, Ruby. It is common to feel and think as you do. You're not a robot, Ruby. You're a special educator, and this is when the focus must shift from you to the students' needs. Teaching is not a performance to be reviewed; it is an act of communication and commitment where you are leading the dance. We can help you find your rhythm."

Leader

Mr. Ford ended the call and sighed. A parent had phoned to lodge a complaint against special educator Ruby. "My child isn't getting the support he needs or the time we were promised. He is getting a diluted version of the curriculum. That is *not* what he needs."

As a parent himself, Mr. Ford appreciated the caller's polite yet powerful words. As a principal, he wondered again why people always felt they would be better teachers than the ones holding the positions. Was it because they had all attended school?

Public opinion aside, Ford was committed to helping Ruby succeed. Ford recognized that the effort to develop Ruby's skills as a teacher provided an opportunity to foster epistemic empathy. He had known Ruby since she was a child, when he'd coached her soccer team. He knew her capacity for caring but realized that it was getting lost in her anxiety—fears of being a new teacher, fear of speaking to parents. He knew Ruby had a need to be in control, a need to be right. Although they were in the midst of piloting a program to strengthen epistemic empathy, Ford acknowledged that he'd not been using it himself to work with Ruby. He'd neglected his responsibility to the newbie almost as soon as he'd assigned Rosemary Rok as Ruby's mentor teacher. Rosemary was a gifted teacher; not only did her students excel, they loved her, as did the rest of the faculty, many of whom she'd guided during their careers. He'd just assumed Rosemary would take care of any problems. Ford was in his third year as administrator; he felt empathy for the novice because he, too, had unmet expectations. There were many days when he got bogged down with the details of running a school. His reaction to stress made him behave abruptly, and the teachers were somewhat cautious around him, he knew. He had so hoped to establish a collaborative atmosphere. Ford thought, and not for the first time, that schools would improve if everyone were to walk in each other's shoes for a while.

Ford was an expert in curriculum design. During his interview for the leadership slot, he'd described a school where differentiation was the driving principle, and technology was creatively employed to enhance learning. He'd promised to build a learning community where families were invited to enhance the curriculum, where teachers were encouraged to find their best selves in designing effective instruction.

The phone rang again. It was the superintendent calling.

"Dr. Powers! How are things at Central Office today?" Ford asked and tried to assume the supe's perspective as he listened to the reply.

As you read the chapters in Crossing II, continue to build your epistemic empathy. Consider the content from the varied perspectives of Ruby, Ms. Rok, Mr. Ford, and other participants. What differing perspectives will they bring to curriculum and assessment? How will the assessment impact their roles differently? What opportunities and challenges will each find in building culturally responsive pedagogy? How will each ensure that students are taught social and emotional skills? At the conclusion of each chapter, complete the Epistemic Empathy Exercise, which will post an unstructured problem reflecting on the knowledge and skills addressed in the chapter.

CHAPTER 4

Curriculum and Assessment

Curriculum and assessment are foundational road maps for student learning. Curriculum outlines what students learn, and assessment determines whether they've learned it. Curriculum standards are helpful in identifying the skills and knowledge expected of students at different moments as they progress through school. They provide guidance for assessment. The curriculum, bound by standards, can be multifaceted. While standards target knowledge and skills expected of successful students, the standards do not encompass the additional learning that takes place in schools. Although content may seem well defined by the written curriculum, there may be additional skills and perceptions students are expected to grasp that are not specified in the documentation. Students with special needs often require support to access the many layers of the curriculum. Enhanced strategies, supplementary materials, assistive technology, and authentic assessment are tools special educators need to scaffold curriculum and assessment for their students.

APPLYING STANDARDS TO SPECIAL EDUCATION

Academic standards apply to special education. ESSA requires that 99% of students in special education follow state achievement standards while 1% may follow alternative standards, and these standards must be aligned with the state standards (Agoratus, 2016). Novice special educators, therefore, need an understanding of their state academic standards. Polloway et al. (2018) emphasized the importance of special educators in linking the standards to functionality for their students. For example, a goal focusing on vocabulary development becomes functional when students learn vocabulary that is a match for their needs, such as occupational vocabulary (Patton & Trainor, 2002). The Individualized Education Plan (IEP) serves as a guide to blending standards with function for students with disabilities.

Equal access to standards is supported when special educators collaborate with general education teachers. Teachers can be proactive by following the three principles of Universal Design for Learning (UDL): multiple means of representation (ways to acquire information), multiple means of expression (ways to demonstrate understanding), and multiple means of engagement (ways to increase motivation).

Using UDL to develop standards-based lessons is a two-part process. Part one is unwrapping the standard (Ainsworth, 2003) and part two is applying UDL guidelines to the lesson (Rao & Meo, 2016). Teachers *unwrap the standard* by identifying the core skills and concepts addressed by a given standard. Teachers can then collaborate to consider the lesson goals, assessments, methods, and materials framed with UDL (Rao & Meo, 2016).

Along with UDL, *evidence-based instructional strategies* are also key for students with disabilities to attain standards. The use of explicit instruction with frequent monitoring has been proven effective (McLaughlin, 2012). Having addressed the integration of standards and requirements of the IEP, the special educator would do well to develop a sound understanding of the general education curriculum.

MEETING CHALLENGES OF THE GENERAL EDUCATION CURRICULUM

According to Nolet and McLaughlin (2005), ensuring access to the general education curriculum should be the cornerstone of a student's IEP. Within the IEP, the specified special education and related services move the student forward in the general education curriculum. To accomplish this the novice special educator needs to be proficient in three areas of teaching: knowledge of content subject matter, understanding how students learn, and designing instruction. A clear understanding of what makes up the general education curriculum is needed to be able to integrate these three components of teaching so that students with disabilities have access to the curriculum.

Remillard (2016) provides guidelines for teachers to analyze the curriculum. Publishers' criteria for the Common Core State Standards have been established and even specified according to content area (Coleman & Pimentel, 2012a, 2012b; Common Core State Standards–Mathematics, 2012). These are available for review for the special educator to see the connections to the general education curriculum and the standards. When special educators review their school curricula, they will identify the larger concepts and see how accommodations might be made to help their students access these concepts. Next, the teacher may review lesson sequence to see where further planning is required. Teachers may even be able to predict where in the curriculum unexpected responses to the lesson will generate alternative teaching and response strategies. Lastly, collaboration with colleagues to gain insight and additional strategies as well as promote school-wide curriculum coherence will be beneficial.

Three aspects of the general education curriculum are important for the novice special educator to grapple with when planning access for students with IEPs. These are explicit, hidden, and absent curricula (Schubert, 1993).

Explicit or intended curriculum. The *explicit* or intended curriculum is the standards-based general education curriculum. Most states have state curriculum frameworks that include the subject matter domains, benchmarks and objectives by grade level. These curriculum frameworks drive the course content that is taught. Many state assessments are linked directly to these frameworks. The student's IEP makes the intended curriculum accessible (Nolet & McLaughlin, 2005).

Hidden or taught curriculum. The *hidden* curriculum, or taught curriculum, is where the explicit general education curriculum is operationalized. This captures more than just the lessons and activities. It includes all the instructional strategies the special educator will use, such as explicit instruction, scaffolded supports, flexible grouping, active engagement, assistive technology, intensive instruction, and constructive feedback (McLeskey et al., 2019). The materials the teachers use, time on topics, activities, and how students will use the information are also part of the taught curriculum. While the IEP is viewed as the taught curriculum, it is helpful to students if the teachers expand upon it (Nolet & McLaughlin, 2005). Integration of curriculum and IEP is vital.

Absent or learned curriculum. The *absent* curriculum, or learned curriculum, is what students actually take away from the learning environment. This will include more than the skills and knowledge from the intended curriculum. For example, some students with disabilities may learn "helplessness" from failing to succeed in the instructional setting. Teachers who are apprehensive about mathematics may convey this anxiety to their students. Students may take away unintended inaccuracies and misinformation (Nolet & McLaughlin, 2005). It is necessary for teachers to be aware of explicit, hidden, and absent curricula when planning for students with IEPs (Polloway et al., 2018).

REVIEWING SPECIALIZED CURRICULUM AND ASSISTIVE TECHNOLOGY

To fully grasp the general curriculum, some students in special education will benefit from specific curriculum and technology. Listed below are some commonly used specialized curricula in reading, mathematics, writing, and functional skills. While curriculum in social-emotional learning has not been exclusively designed for students with disabilities, there are programs that support social and emotional growth for all students. Some students in special education access curriculum via assistive technology. IDEA requires that assistive technology be addressed in the IEP. The resources (Tables 4.1–4.5) that follow have strong peer-review support.

Assistive Technology for the Classroom

Assistive technology, broadly, refers to materials used to assist student learning. Teachers may use a variety of technologies from "high" tech, such as adaptive switches, to "low" tech, such as pencil grips. Listed below are a variety of assistive technology devices.

- Voice-recognition software—allows students capability to dictate responses
- C-Pen Reader—reads text aloud and can display a word definition
- Highlighters—assist in reading and writing
- Color overlays—facilitate reading
- Teacher FM systems—coordinate communication via radio wave improving reception for students with hearing impairments
- Adaptive switches—accommodate students with fine motor challenges
- Writing software—increases effectiveness for student composition by correcting mechanics
- Slant boards or pencil grips—ease physical requirements for student writing

(continued on page 50)

Table 4.1. Specialized Reading

Resource	Description	URL Link
Wilson Reading System	Intensive structured, multisensory literacy approach	https://www.wilsonlanguage.com/programs/wilson-reading-system/
Fundations	Multisensory approach to language programs including phonics, vocabulary, fluency, comprehension, writing, and spelling grades K–3	https://www.wilsonlanguage.com/programs/fundations/
Just Words	Explicit, multisensory approach in decoding and spelling grades 4–12	https://www.wilsonlanguage.com/programs/just-words/
The Edmark Reading Program	Highly repetitive word recognition approach that is systematic and uses an errorless learning approach	https://www.proedinc.com/Products/13620/edmark-reading-program-level-1--second-edition-complete-kit.aspx
Orton-Gillingham Approach	Explicit, sequentially structured, multisensory approach to teaching literacy by an experienced teacher	https://www.orton-gillingham.com/

Table 4.2. Specialized Mathematics

Resource	Description	URL Link
TouchMath	A tactile, multisensory approach to math for grades pre-K–3 focused on numbers and operations	https://www.touchmath.com/
Corrective Math	Direct instruction in basic mathematic areas	https://www.mheducation.com/prek-12/program/corrective-math-20052005/MKTSP-UVI02M0.html?page=1&sortby=title&order=asc&bu=seg

Table 4.3. Specialized Writing

Resource	Description	URL Link
Handwriting Without Tears	Multisensory, unique letter order approach for early writing for grades K–5	https://www.lwtears.com/hwt
Keyboarding Without Tears	Color-coded approach to keyboarding	https://www.lwtears.com/kwt

Table 4.4. Functional Skills Curriculum

Resource	Description	URL Link
Enhance: Functional Life Skills	Print and software grades 6–12 survival guides for community life and personal care	https://www.attainmentcompany.com
Life Centered Education (LCE) Transition Curriculum	Focus on daily living, self-determination and interpersonal skills as well as employment skills	https://www.cec.sped.org/Publications/LCE-Transition-Curriculum

Table 4.5. Social Emotional Curriculum

Resource	Description	URL Link
Open Circle	Develops a safe community and problem solving with curriculum at all levels	https://www.open-circle.org/our-approach/curriculum
Responsive Classroom	Student-centered focus on academics, community, management based on developmental awareness to develop social skills and academic mindset	https://www.responsiveclassroom.org/
Superflex . . . A Superhero Social Thinking Curriculum	Focuses on self-regulation curriculum for young students	https://www.socialthinking.com/Products/superflex-superhero-social-thinking-curriculum
Zones of Regulation	Teaches self-regulation by categorizing how we feel and states of alertness into four zones	https://www.zonesofregulation.com/learn-more-about-the-zones.html

- Graphic organizers or specially lined paper—display logical relationships among ideas through visual representation
- Calculators—eliminate cognitive requirement for basic mathematical operations
- Vibrating watch—reminds students to attend to learning
- Video self-monitoring—illustrates students in desirable circumstances or illustrates behaviors targeted for change
- Pictorial software—provides visual representations for interventions including visual schedules and Social Stories

ASSESSING STUDENT PROGRESS TOWARD MEETING THE STANDARDS

To assess performance in general education curriculum or specialized curriculum, criterion-referenced tests (CRTs) are useful. CRTs report how students are doing relative to predetermined performance goals on school, district, or state curriculum (Pierangelo & Guiliani, 2017).

Direct measures of academic skills that are tied directly to instructional curriculum are often used. Curriculum-based assessment (CBA) is used to measure student mastery on grade-level curriculum or adapted curriculum based on a student's IEP goals. CBA is an ongoing process of monitoring students' strengths, interests, and emerging skills going into the curriculum and throughout the school career (Pierangelo & Guiliani, 2017).

Curriculum-based measurement (CBM) allows teachers and students to monitor performance. CBM is a visual depiction of student progress through graphing data. This helps students and teachers identify what is working and when change should be made (Kritikos et al., 2018).

In some circumstances, test accommodations and modifications or alternative measures are used with students with disabilities (Kritikos et al., 2018). A section in the IEP addresses test accommodations for the student. Erickson et al. (1998) divide testing accommodations into four types: timing, setting, presentation, and response. Accommodations such as extended time, quiet setting, having directions read, or providing oral responses rather than written may be included.

Some students in special education require progress monitoring through alternative assessments where teachers compile information in portfolios, often from performance-based assessments (Almond & Case, 2004). Sir (2017) compared two alternative assessment systems,

Dynamic Learning Maps (DLM) and the Multi-State Alternative Assessment (MSAA). DLM is a learning map model that takes academic content standards and illustrates the interplay of knowledge, incremental skills, and understandings. It is a way to view the student on a continuum. It provides measurements in English language arts, mathematics, and science, meeting statutory requirements to report all student achievement. The DLM alternative assessment system also provides data to guide instruction and inform parents. The MSAA is the other widely used alternative assessment system. It was developed for students with significant cognitive delays in grades 3 through 8 and grade 11. It assesses skills in English language arts and mathematics. This assessment may be accessed through paper/pencil, online, or by hybrid techniques. It contains multiple choice and constructive response items.

The intention of special education is inclusion, to keep the student's experience as similar as possible to that of typical students. The flexibility of teachers and students helps make this possible.

EPISTEMIC EMPATHY EXERCISE

"Patience!" Ruby whispered to herself. Johnathan's mother was here again. Ruby knew family involvement was important; she knew it was beneficial to the students, but her stomach sank when in strode the mother, file folder in hand.

Johnathan's mother was a force to reckon with. She coddled her son to extremes. Because he was obese, she insisted on a special size desk with a rocking chair so he could easily stand up. Because he had a processing issue, she demanded the most current software. IEP meetings were trying. Johnathan's mom dominated the first 20 minutes or so as she shared, repeatedly, the story of his difficult birth, and subsequent episodes that demonstrated his superior nature. Ruby knew it was wrong, but she often joined in on the eye-rolling and sighing.

Today's meeting was to center around specialized curriculum for Johnathan as well as the state assessment. Johnathan had achieved a B last quarter in math, and his mother had researched a specialized curriculum package that promised to lead her son to mastery. In addition, Mom wanted to petition for alternate assessment due to Johnathan's anxiety and physical limitations.

Ruby was uncomfortable meeting alone with this mom whose superpower was persuasion. So Mr. Ford and Ms. Rok had already come to the conference table when Ruby entered the office.

BRIDGE BUILDER

The graphic organizer below will help you structure your discussion of the issue presented in the Epistemic Empathy Exercise. In the left column are listed the persons involved in the dilemma. Respond to the questions in the right column as the designated person would respond. Use epistemic empathy; take the perspective of another in order to analyze the issue. Collaborate to solve the problem.

Ruby	What did Ms. Rok think when I asked her to join the meeting?
	How can I get Mr. Ford to support me in this meeting?
Mr. Ford	Why is Ruby so concerned about this meeting?
	How does Ms. Rok interact with this parent?
Ms. Rok	What happened that made Ruby so nervous about this parent meeting?
	What will Mr. Ford think about being invited to this meeting?
Collaborative Solution	How can the team *investigate* specialized curriculum programs for this student?
	How can the team *determine* if the student needs accommodations on the state testing?

CHAPTER 5

Culturally Responsive Pedagogy

Ensuring learning for all students has always been the goal of special educators. Accommodating students' differences by altering instruction and curricula to meet their needs is the core of the profession. Such inclusive practices, originally developed to accommodate students with learning differences, may be interpreted more broadly to apply to the effective instruction of students with cultural and linguistic differences (Brown, 2007). When students with cognitive differences are provided with scaffolding to access the curricula, interact socially, and work with typically developing students, inclusion is achieved.

Demographics are shifting. In 2020, students of historically underrepresented groups will make up 50% of classroom population (Chen, 2019). These students bring perspectives and practices that differ greatly from those of most teachers in the field. Pedagogy must ameliorate this gap. Teachers will only be effective if they build bridges between that which they have known and experienced and that which their students have known and experienced (Howard, 2007; Villegas & Lucas, 2002).

Epistemic empathy is vital to this endeavor. As special educators work to understand the thinking of their students in terms of cognition, so, too, might they learn to anticipate, recognize, and incorporate their students' linguistic and cultural perspectives. It is this awareness of the individual student's needs and experiences that forms the bridge between special education and culturally responsive pedagogy (Griner & Stewart, 2013).

Opportunities for teachers to practice culturally responsive teaching abound, but research points to four areas where CRP is vital: classroom climate, communication, learning strategies, and behavior management (Howard, 2012).

ESTABLISHING CLASSROOM CLIMATE

It has been established that social interaction enhances learning (Moll, 2006). When learners work together, in zones of proximal development, they can increase children's cognitive and social development (Cesar & Santos, 2006). In a culturally responsive classroom, teachers have the power to scaffold such interaction by developing a welcoming environment. A welcoming classroom climate may be established in a variety of ways, some of which are suggested below:

- Smile at students as soon as they arrive. This is their classroom, so you want students to feel comfortable and part of the community.
- Provide visual supports. Picture schedules will help them follow the sequence of the day. Common objects may be labeled in a variety of languages.
- Ensure that all students are represented around the room. Be sure there are readily available pictures and books that refer to their experiences.
- Introduce them to several helpful peers: "knowledgeable others." Suggest games and activities that have universal appeal. Provide appropriate materials for students to share.
- Avoid assumptions. Guard against imposing expectations on newcomers. For example, some students may have had interrupted formal educations, and the sequence of the day may not be familiar. Others may have been educated in formal systems where students are not welcome to speak. Take your time and observe. When are the students comfortable? When is their behavior unexpected? Plan instruction around what you learn from your observations.
- Hold high expectations. This is one tenet from special education that resonates in regard to culturally responsive pedagogy. Once you've provided the scaffolding and accommodations, your students are expected to produce. To expect otherwise is to suggest that they are incapable. Holding high expectations is a matter of respect.
- Educate yourself. Learn all you can about different cultures, attitudes, beliefs and practices, especially those of the students in front of you (Deady, 2017).

FOSTERING COMMUNICATION

The second area of opportunity for culturally responsive pedagogy centers around communication. Communication in education has traditionally been considered in terms of the presentation of new material. Care is given to that which is being said, and how it is being said. However, in working with students with disabilities, Council for Exceptional Children (CEC) standards focus increasingly on the importance of listening to students. Listening tells teachers what the student knows and doesn't know and where the student's thinking derails. Listening to students from culturally and linguistically diverse (CLD) backgrounds also provides vital information.

Students from CLD backgrounds present a wide variety of ways of communicating. Some students have learned to respond to questions succinctly, while others embed their responses in narrative. Students from some cultures maintain formal relationships with their teachers while others are more informal than is common in U.S. classrooms. These different ways of communicating certainly impact learning. In welcoming culturally and linguistically diverse students, good teachers will be flexible enough to recognize different patterns of communication.

When working with English learners, basic principles of second language acquisition apply. Learning a second language may take up to ten years and is a developmental process. Students first learn basic interpersonal communication skills (BICS). Although these skills allow students to chat outside class, they may not speak for up to a year in the formal setting. This is known as the silent period. Students gain cognitive academic language proficiency (CALP) as their engagement in the curriculum is enhanced (Cummins, 2008). CALP continues to develop throughout the student's academic career.

The U.S. government has provided a website to assist teachers in working with communication challenges presented by English learners. WIDA.us presents standards for English learners. The standards are interpreted in terms of subjects, grades, ages, and language proficiency across the domains of listening, speaking, reading, and writing. The emphasis of the website is on providing teachers with assistance so that English learners can build their English skills while pursuing subject knowledge.

Effective communication is imperative when working with families of students from culturally and linguistically diverse backgrounds.

The most impactful approach is to learn about the relationships to school experienced by the students and their families. Parents and guardians may not know the protocols and practices common in local classrooms. It is up to the teacher to extend a welcoming climate to families (Breiseth, 2016). Culturally responsive practices for effectively communicating with parents of diverse learners are listed below:

- Initiate communication by sending a note, making a phone call, or visiting the family if appropriate.
- Invite the family members to school. Allow them to participate at their own pace but let them know they have value to add to all students' learning.
- Use visuals to communicate. Send photos of their students working during the day.
- Send home photos of materials chosen to reflect the student's experiences.
- Contact or meet with families when their students experience success.
- Provide an agenda to the family members several days in advance. Use objective, measured language. Include the goal of the meeting in advance.
- Respect differences. Most likely, families will demonstrate attitudes similar to their students' attitudes—toward punctuality, language used with authority figures, body language, attitude toward school. While focusing on the intended outcome of the meeting, expect and respect differences in communication styles.

Through experiences communicating with students and their families, teachers have many opportunities to incorporate culturally responsive practices (Howard, 2007).

PROMOTING LEARNING STRATEGIES

Planning and teaching provide another avenue for incorporating culturally responsive pedagogy. Students learn differently, and individual needs must be accommodated. Special educators embrace this notion. However, differences are not limited to cognitive preferences and abilities. Students from culturally and linguistically diverse backgrounds have often experienced different avenues for learning, and effective teachers learn to embrace this variety of backgrounds (Wlodkowski & Ginsberg, 1995). Instructional decisions, often using backward design, are constantly being made by teachers scaffolding learning (Wiggins & McTighe, 2005). The choices listed below may be impacted by students' experiences, and suggestions are provided for reflecting cultural and linguistic diversity.

Objectives: The statement of what the student will know and be able to do may be profoundly impacted by culture. Is the objective culturally biased? Does it require background information the students may not have? Is the amount of time dedicated to the objective appropriate given culture and language?

Assessment: How will the student demonstrate the attainment of the objective? Is the student's attitude toward demonstration impacted by culture? Is the student's demonstration of knowledge hampered by language? Is the assessment too individualistic for a student from a community-focused background?

Materials: Can the student access the materials? Is an avenue available for every student to access materials regardless of disability or language? Does the student understand the use of concrete objects in the lesson? Are the materials culturally bound, or are they equally familiar to all students?

Technology: Does the student have experience with forms of technology? Will the technology improve or impede access to the curriculum? Can technology bridge the cultural and linguistic divide, or will it increase the gap?

Explicit Instruction: Presentation of information is culturally bound. It is a form of communication and reflects the mores and practices of the speaker. Will the students be able to glean the most important information despite stylistic differences? Might the teacher support explicit instruction with materials to reinforce the presentation?

Grouping: Although a basic premise of this work is the value of social interaction for learning, cultures interact differently. What grouping practices work best for students from varied backgrounds? Has the teacher made clear the purpose for the grouping choices? Do the students have any say?

Assignments: Out of class learning is valuable and relevant, but it can take many forms. Teachers develop assignments so that students may review or explore, affirm or question their learning. The teacher must reflect on the background information the assignment requires, the time and materials expected, the locus of control. Is the assignment a personal exploration for the student? An extension of learning? These decisions must be made clear to students who may have experienced very different assignments, including rote learning and practice.

Questioning: An invaluable tool for assessing learning, questioning is a basic strategy and tool for teachers. Following Bloom's taxonomy, a teacher may ramp up learning just by asking strategic questions. However, questioning reflects cultural and communication habits. Each teacher must reflect on culture's role in questioning—is it too direct, too rapid fire? Is wait time the same across cultures? What if the student dissembles? What if the student is incorrect? Will the teacher's responses take culture into consideration?

Study Strategies: All students need scaffolding for learning how to learn. Those from culturally and linguistically diverse backgrounds may need additional assistance. Do the students know what kind of information is valued? Is the goal to learn discrete facts or broad concepts? Are students expected to give back what they've learned? Are they supposed to have gone further independently? Teachers must clarify for diverse students exact expectations for learning, and strategies for accomplishing that goal.

Social–emotional learning has gained legitimacy in American classrooms. Teachers are imbuing students' content learning with opportunities to develop skills to manage emotions and build empathetic relationships. Students whose experiences with school have not included such learning may be confused by its presence. Furthermore, families may not anticipate that schooling will include these attributes. It is important that the teacher introduce this concept to families upon their enrollment in the school community. Families must be assured that these interpersonal skills are not culturally dependent; rather, they are best practices for participating in the classroom. Students should be encouraged to discuss the differences between their social and emotional development and what they are experiencing in the classroom.

In sum, lessons that attend to cultural and linguistic differences will be more effective for diverse learners. The broad suggestions listed above will help teachers reflect on their culturally responsive practices as they plan learning activities.

UNDERSTANDING BEHAVIOR MANAGEMENT

The final area where culturally responsive pedagogy is a must is that of behavior management. Behavior is deeply rooted in culture, and its expression reveals the values held by that culture. Behavior that is encouraged and applauded in one culture may be prohibited in another. This can be very difficult for teachers and confusing for students. For students who are not cultural natives, the hidden curriculum may disrupt learning and success. Think about the complexity of the messages a newcomer might receive. Is he to speak up? Speak when spoken to? Not interrupt? Contribute to the classroom conversation? What are the rules?

The most important aspect of CRP as it relates to behavior management is consistency. Teacher and students must work together to develop a lexicon for expected behaviors. Such shared determination allows the students to listen and talk until they understand the expectation, and to understand the consequences when the rules are breached. Concrete suggestions for teachers are listed below:

- Model expected behavior with examples and non-examples.
- Encourage students to role-play using examples and non-examples.
- Determine rules for the classroom together.
- Post the rules in several places.
- Discuss and practice daily until the expectation is part of the routine.
- Be consistent in addressing infractions immediately with appropriate consequences.
- Acknowledge your own mistakes and misinterpretations and discuss with the student.

Best practices in culturally responsive pedagogy focus on the individual student, similar to the focus in special education. In both cases, an effective teacher responds to students' culture experiences, interests, and cognitive processes to develop instruction. To design learning according to the students' perspective is to use epistemic empathy.

EPISTEMIC EMPATHY EXERCISE

Ms. Rok and Will Ford were speaking in hushed tones as Ruby entered the office. As she approached the group, its third member rose to greet her. The man, dressed conservatively and formal in manner, was introduced as the parent of a new student to whom Ruby had been alerted, Ty. Ruby was following his progress closely.

Ty's father, Mr. Abel, was deferential to Ruby, asking for her input and her impressions of the child. As she spoke, he seemed to listen intently. When she completed her brief analysis, he nodded thoughtfully and said, "You are all amazing teachers, and you're the ones who will make it possible for Ty to graduate at the top of his class. I'd like to support your efforts by providing you with laptops for every student in this school. Furthermore, I'd like to hire you, Ruby, to tutor Ty on weekends and during the summer. I'll pay you anything you'd like."

Ruby was about to refuse outright, but Mr. Ford stood up, thanked Mr. Abel, and said they'd be in touch. Ruby was shocked. Ms. Rok could not maintain eye contact. Mr. Ford was ecstatic. What do you think happened next?

BRIDGE BUILDER

The graphic organizer below will help you structure your discussion of the issue presented in the Epistemic Empathy Exercise. In the left column are listed the persons involved in the dilemma. Respond to the questions in the right column as the designated person would respond. Use epistemic empathy; take the perspective of another in order to analyze the issue. Collaborate to solve the problem.

Ruby	What did Ms. Rok think when Mr. Abel offered me the tutoring position? Why did Mr. Ford stand up so abruptly?
Mr. Ford	Why is Ruby so upset about the tutoring offer? How does Ms. Rok feel about this situation?
Ms. Rok	How can I support Ruby in this unusual situation? What will Mr. Ford say once Mr. Abel leaves?
Collaborative Solution	How can the team *determine* the best course of action to support the generous parent but still maintain proper boundaries? As a team, how will you *get going*? What will be your next steps and roles for each team member?

CHAPTER 6

Social and Emotional Learning

Encouraging epistemic empathy among special educators may very well strengthen the profession, but its value isn't limited to the professionals. Teaching epistemic empathy to students is just as important. The topics and issues reviewed in earlier chapters are vital for the effective teaching of students with special needs, but the knowledge and skills that may be most impactful for students are those associated with social and emotional learning. Social interaction supports learning. Students need to be taught how to develop and manage social interaction. Strong social and emotional skills provide students with the flexibility they need to navigate varied situations. An effective special educator will recognize where to focus, how to structure learning, and how to encourage the development of social and emotional learning.

The ability of special educators to persist and thrive rests heavily on social interaction and epistemic empathy, and so may the success of students with special needs. Emphasis has rightly been given to exploring effective strategies to support students' academic learning, but effective strategies for students to use in developing effective relationships are equally important. Clearly, students with disabilities need social and emotional learning to increase their receptivity to academic learning, but they also benefit by increasing their effectiveness in developing sound relationships.

The recent focus on social and emotional learning has not been limited to the field of special education. In fact, attention to this effort has been widespread and thorough. Standards and curricula have been disseminated by the Collaborative for Academic, Social, and Emotional Learning (CASEL). Their website provides a plethora of ideas and approaches useful in the classroom. Attention is given to helping students develop competency in the following areas: self-awareness, self-management, social awareness, relationship skills, and responsible decisionmaking (casel.org/what-is-sel/). These competencies are valuable across cultures and abilities. Research shows that skills in these areas improve students' academic, personal, and social experiences (Frey et al., 2019).

Suggestions for Integrating Social and Emotional Learning

- Employ direct instruction of skills.
- Model appropriate behavior.
- Display relevant materials.
- Identify skills as they are being used.
- Incorporate activities and discussions related to the competencies.
- Develop classroom norms or expectations for group work.
- Model and teach active listening skills, turn-taking and compromise. Have anchor charts visible to teach these skills.
- Conduct fishbowl exercises and role-play situations that involve conflict (Frey et al., 2019).

DEVELOPING EMPATHY

Empathy is the ability of one person to assume the *feelings* of another; epistemic empathy expands that concept to include the assumption of the *perspectives* of another. The former highlights affective reactions, and the latter includes understanding the way another person thinks. Epistemic empathy is important for students with and without disabilities as well as for their teachers.

One way to teach empathy is through literature. Classrooms should have literature that represents different cultures and abilities. Reading together provides a wonderful opportunity to begin conversations about how different characters in the book feel and react to different situations.

Additional Suggestions for Promoting Empathy

- Have students switch name tags and assume the thinking skill of the person whose name they assume.
- Ask students to predict questions others may ask.
- Allow students to respond to interview questions through the voice of another.
- Require students to write alternative descriptions or endings from a different character's point of view.
- Select a classroom library with books from diverse cultures.

ENGENDERING SELF-DETERMINATION

Self-determination refers to the individual's ability to achieve goals by identifying and taking appropriate action (Field & Hoffman, 2012). Teachers can take an active role in helping students develop self-determination. Wehmeyer (1996) outlines 11 skills and attributes of self-determination: choice making, decisionmaking, problem solving, goal setting, self-management, self-advocacy, leadership, internal locus of control, positive outcome expectancy, self-awareness, and self-knowledge. Teachers can provide opportunities for students to work on these skills daily in the classroom and school community.

The special educator can provide students with disabilities opportunity to set goals and problem-solve. This can involve choice. When students have a role in their own IEP development, they are provided an opportunity for self-advocacy, which also encourages leadership (Salend, 2016). Teachers can help students analyze the actions that lead to success or failure and use this information to plan their learning. Students taking responsibility for their own learning is an example of internal locus of control (Boykin & Noguera, 2011). When a student has voice in making decisions about learning, the student owns the decision. The student has the power.

TEACHING STUDENTS WHO HAVE EXPERIENCED TRAUMA

Supporting students in their self-advocacy and teaching students social and emotional skills are powerful tools for leading students to independence. However, some students have experienced roadblocks that interfere with their social and emotional progress. Twenty-six percent of students will experience trauma before the age of 4 (Craig, 2016). Most teachers will have students in their classrooms who have endured some type of trauma. Students who have experienced trauma may not be focused on social and emotional learning. In fact, in class they may exhibit behaviors that are not social, and not emotionally sound. Educators cannot take students' behavior personally. It is often a reaction to something that happened earlier in the student's life. The teacher's job, when working with students who have experienced trauma, is to help those students regulate their emotions.

Children may try to reenact the trauma that they experience. It is essential that the teacher recognize this and respond in a calm and respectful manner. Such equanimity will help the student feel safe with the teacher and develop a trusting relationship. A teacher with consistent and orderly routines is providing a safe environment. Students need to be warned when changes to the routine are anticipated. Disruptions to the routine can be upsetting to students who need the routine to feel safe.

Many teachers who work with students who have experienced trauma include self-regulation activities in their daily plans. Meditations, deep breathing exercises and yoga become part of the students' routines. Movement breaks and energizers are also beneficial to keep students engaged and on task. When students can tell that the teacher values their feelings and is trying to include activities that will make them successful, students will be motivated to do their best work (Craig, 2016).

Suggestions for Assisting Student with Trauma

- Include self-regulation strategies for the whole class: starting lessons with deep breathing, using guided meditation after recess.
- Keep a visual schedule of the day's planned sequence and be sure to update it with any changes.
- Incorporate movement into lessons. Examples: learning stations, museum walk, and inside outside circle.
- Provide sensory items for students to channel their restlessness.
- Check in with students to see how they are feeling each day.

BUILDING SOCIAL AND EMOTIONAL SKILLS OUTSIDE THE CLASSROOM

Supporting students with disabilities while keeping them genuinely included in the classroom is a major goal of special education. However, it is often outside of the classroom where students with disabilities feel most excluded (Coster et al., 2013). Efforts to include students with disabilities outside the classroom have increased during the last several years. The movement toward Unified Sports and Unified Arts has provided a pathway for students with disabilities to extend their engagement with others outside the classroom (Sullivan & Glidden, 2014). While school districts and teachers can scaffold students' participation in co-curricular activities, the full value is achieved if the students are included socially and not just as parallel participants. The areas listed below, organized around social and emotional competencies, are of particular relevance to students with special needs. Mastery of these skills will allow students with special needs to achieve greater inclusion in co-curricular settings and may be used as instructional goals by the teacher.

Self-Awareness

- Maintaining appropriate personal space
- Attending to proper hygiene
- Modulating volume of voice
- Applying appropriate level of attention

Self-Management

- Being punctual and using time effectively
- Arranging personal and task-oriented materials and tools
- Using appropriate body language and facial expression during conversation and collaboration
- Controlling emotional reactions

Social Awareness

- Activating empathy
- Contributing appropriately to conversation and collaboration
- Learning about the topic ahead of time
- Reading body language and tone of others

Relationship Building

- Treating others with respect
- Actively listening to others' input
- Managing appropriate communication with other participants as follow-up to the event
- Being interested in the lives of others

Responsible Decisionmaking

- Recognizing when and how to self-advocate
- Learning how to evaluate information from different sources
- Articulating consequences for decisions made
- Understanding when to seek help from leaders

These areas may pose challenges for students with disabilities in the areas of social and emotional learning. Students with special needs benefit from direct instruction of and practice with these areas in order to be increasingly successful in out-of-classroom situations.

Finally, the tenets of social and emotional learning are increasingly meaningful to students with and without disabilities as they transition from school. Whether headed to postsecondary settings, work, or another form of daily interaction, students with and without disabilities transfer not only academic knowledge and skills, but social and emotional principles and practices as well. As students approach emancipation from special education, they and their guardians participate in transition planning. Special educators arrange for carefully planned experiences for the students as they draw closer to the adult world. Transition plans anticipate the needs of students across environments including work and leisure. When done well, transition plans include goals that consider the student's interests, strengths and challenges, and dreams. As the student nears graduation, she or he is provided with opportunities to practice vocational skills. It is just as important that the transition plan build in opportunities to practice social and emotional skills. Students with disabilities are underemployed and do not graduate from college in anticipated numbers (Thomas & Dykes, 2011). They are often left without structures for social inclusion once they leave school. By instructing and practicing social and emotional learning, special educators have the privilege of being able to assist students in planning for these eventualities. A student who has learned to find a friend, make a friend, and be a friend, is a student who has increased likelihood of being included.

EPISTEMIC EMPATHY EXERCISE

The general education teacher, John, wrote to ask Ruby for an appointment to discuss a situation that was impacting one of "her" students. Ruby sighed when she read the email. He kept doing that, no matter how many times Ruby rephrased the singular possessive to the plural. It seemed like Ruby wove in conversation about "our students" until she no longer had breath. She responded to the email, agreeing to meet early the next morning. As always, she was ready to advocate for the kids on her caseload.

John arrived promptly at 7:00 a.m., with two cups of coffee. Ruby found this act of cordiality disarming, and she relaxed a bit as her colleague began to speak. He was concerned about repeated incidents of bullying, and Ruby felt an adrenaline rush as she, ironically, readied for battle to protect "her" student. Imagine her surprise when John explained that it was a student with an IEP who was doing the bullying.

Marvin was a student with ASD. He was a polite, serious student. His disability was evidenced by his perseveration, and by his insistence that he was always right. When paired with another student, whose work was less structured (to the point of halfhearted), Marvin turned into a bully. He shamed the other boy for his sloppy work. He repeatedly criticized the boy for not completing tasks. The boy's mother had reached out to John for assistance.

Ruby was stymied. She was chagrined to realize she'd assumed her student would be the victim, the underdog. She'd never before been in this position. Her typical responses were inadequate. In other circumstances, she'd proclaim, "We will educate the gen. ed. students about disabilities," "We will conduct simulation activities," "We will have students work together so they can learn more about each other!" She didn't know what to do next. What was the law? What was the ethical move? She'd need input from Mr. Ford and Ms. Rok.

What do you think happened next?

BRIDGE BUILDER

The graphic organizer below will help you structure your discussion of the issue presented in the Epistemic Empathy Exercise. In the left column are listed the persons involved in the dilemma. Respond to the questions in the right column as the designated person would respond. Use epistemic empathy; take the perspective of another in order to analyze the issue. Collaborate to solve the problem.

Ruby	What will Ms. Rok's advice be for this situation?
	How will Mr. Ford handle this situation?
Mr. Ford	Why is Ruby involving me in this situation?
	How does Ms. Rok support Ruby?
Ms. Rok	How can I support Ruby with this issue?
	What will Mr. Ford say about a student with an IEP being a bully?
Collaborative Solution	How do we *determine* the best course of action to support the student being bullied and the student with a disability?
	As a team, how do we *evaluate* services available for the student with the disability to improve his communication and social skills?

THE MOSTAR BRIDGE

The story of the Mostar Bridge is one of dedication and collaboration. During the war in Bosnia and Herzegovina in 1993 a historic bridge was destroyed. A local leader, believing the bridge represented an important part of local history and culture was determined it should be rebuilt garnering support from international banks and organizations and multiple countries. The new bridge reopened in 2004. The new bridge is a symbol of resilience, fortitude, and collaboration.

As is Ruby, whose story continues with her professional maturation. Ruby takes on leadership roles, first as mentor, then as director of special education. By generating collaboration Ruby provides a bridge for the next generation to cross.

RUBY THRIVES AS MENTOR

"We were all new once." Ruby recalled her mentor's words of wisdom from 12 years earlier. Taking a deep breath, the new mentor teacher knocked on the classroom door. She'd received her first mentor assignment and would be working with this year's group of novice special educators. Rebecca, a new resource teacher, popped up to assist Ruby with her materials. Rebecca and the others looked so young to Ruby. The room fairly sizzled with excitement, confidence, and nerves.

Ruby matched the people to the information she'd gathered. Jack was the one standing behind the others. During his interview, he'd demonstrated great understanding of behavior management, but he was less confident when asked about differentiation for academics. His letter of recommendation noted that he had potential. Ruby wondered what that actually meant.

Then there was Allie, seated in the front, beaming at the mentor. She was going to be a dynamo—filled with creativity and love for children. She bubbled over when telling stories about "her kids." However, when asked about results, Allie proudly announced, "The kids loved their lessons!" Ruby predicted that Allie might need to find a better balance between instruction and assessment. Allie was a delight, and she wanted the students to be excited and engaged, but did she keep track of what they were learning?

Rebecca was clearly the leader of the group, and a bit didactic. At her interview, she rattled off the school's policies and special education law, but did she understand the concepts? Rebecca was marvelous at explaining the assessment cycle, the possibilities of technology, and choosing adaptations, but she showed no examples, no evidence. Rebecca, of course, didn't know that she hadn't been the first choice for her position. The interviewers felt Rebecca to be a bit impersonal, one even calling her aloof. Another interviewer noted that Rebecca responded to the panel's statements by repeatedly saying, "I knew that." So, Ruby felt there were a few red flags regarding the young woman's disposition for teaching. Rebecca demonstrated a strong need to be right.

Ruby reflected on how she'd arrived at this moment. During her 12 years as a practitioner, she had made so many mistakes, and she'd had her share of triumphs. Ruby felt honored to have been selected as mentor teacher. She wanted so much to assist these new colleagues, but not with the traditional seminar approach. In Ruby's experience, learning was best when in situ and with collaboration. She knew that was the direction she'd take. All three of the novices were certified special educators, but the situations they entered would be quite different.

Jack's assignment was the Behavior Management Room. There he'd teach eight students, all at different points in their academics.

Five paraeducators would be present to help manage the students' problematic behaviors. He'd have to build a team, tapping into the skills of the paraeducators. Allie had been assigned as the inclusion teacher for grades 3–5. Ruby was familiar with the general educators in those grades, and two of the three were excellent. The third was currently under review. Finally, Rebecca was the new resource teacher for grades 4–6. Like Jack, she'd be working with several experienced paraeducators.

Ruby had carefully considered her goals and approach for mentoring. Her first goal was to discover the newbies' styles of teaching. She'd obtained that information through the observations she'd conducted during the first few weeks. Her second goal was more elusive. Ruby had envisioned creating a working group where she and the new teachers would share their successes and challenges, their hopes and dreams. But, by October, each of the new teachers had found a reason to skip several of the working group meetings.

Novices

As it turned out, Jack really did have potential. The new behavior teacher was clearly serving as a role model for so many of the boys in the elementary grades. Jack was empathetic, fair, and a wonderful listener. His was a calming, inclusive presence in the playground, at the bus stop, in the cafeteria. However, he was over-reliant on his charm. He did not seem to have any systems in place—behavioral or academic—and Ruby was concerned about his data management. He was excellent on his feet, but where were his plans?

Jack skipped two of the group meetings because he'd been "needed" elsewhere in the school. He was always whizzing around the building—never stopping to really talk. Ruby understood that he was afraid to make a bad impression, but the wall he set up between them made it hard for her to help him. She'd heard that his students were increasingly rowdy and disruptive during academic hours. Ruby worried that Jack didn't recognize the link between instruction in social–emotional skills and behavior problems. Ruby was concerned. He was so close to being a good teacher, but he wasn't there yet.

Ruby watched Allie interacting animatedly with the kids as they worked. The mentor could feel the excitement of the novice who was thrilled to be a teacher. Allie had spent some of her graduation money on stickers, glitter, and prizes. More than anything, Allie wanted her kids to love school. She'd arrived wearing fun teaching sweaters.

She'd excitedly shared her discovery of a perfect pin to match each of the books she planned to read to all the children during the first month. The newbie had shared her story with Ruby.

Allie was from a "teacher family." Her Abuela, Mami, and Tío Estefan were all seasoned veterans. There was a saying in her family, "¡No quejarse de corregir! Es cómo sabemos lo que los niños han aprendido¡" It meant "No complaining about correcting. It's how we know what the children have learned!" Though Allie adored her family members, she secretly felt the notion was old-fashioned. She could tell how well students were learning by their facial expressions and body language. Besides, too much testing would increase anxiety, the very opposite of the effect she intended. Allie was determined to have an impact on the future of her Latinx children; their dropout rate was high. She had insight into Latin cultures that she was happy to share.

When the novices met at the local restaurant for their Friday noodles, out of the sight of their mentor, Allie and Rebecca noticed that Jack seemed crestfallen. They invited him to share his concerns, promising to listen without judgment. Jack described the chaotic behavior of his students that afternoon. Allie quickly suggested that he make some games and provide candy for winners. Rebecca spouted, "Do not punish them if their behavior is a direct result of their disability. That would be unlawful. Read the IEP; it's a contract." That was Rebecca. She knew the law; she knew the policies. When Jack wondered if he should email parents, Rebecca cited the school's policy regarding contact. When Allie suggested a field trip, Rebecca knew the regulations there, too. It seemed like Rebecca was as squared away as a new teacher could be.

It was when Rebecca was alone that she could not block the self-doubt. She was afraid she wasn't good at teaching. She wondered if she'd chosen the right career. People would ask if she loved it, if she loved the kids, if she felt like she was changing lives, and she'd respond enthusiastically. She didn't really feel that enthusiasm. As she'd prepped for her first position, Rebecca had relied on knowing the regulations, policies, laws. She could recite each required element of an IEP. She felt if she could just follow what others had set before her, she'd be fine. Rebecca could rattle off the rules, but she couldn't connect them to those precious children sitting before her. The IEPs she read left her with more questions than answers. Why was this going so badly?

This was school, and school had always been where Rebecca shone. During all those years of foster care, Rebecca had considered school her safe haven. Rebecca's mom had succumbed to a virus when the child was 8 years old, and she'd gone into the "system." Rebecca had been placed with four families over the years, each dysfunctional in its own way. She'd coped by pouring all her energies into the one aspect of life she could control, academic achievement. Mastering content gave Rebecca some leverage in her otherwise chaotic life. She'd learned that being the best student garnered her the praise she craved, and her pursuit of excellence continued throughout her teacher preparation program. Rebecca had graduated at the top of her class. However, faced with the realities of classroom teaching, Rebecca was finding that her command of the content was not enough.

Each new teacher wanted help; each new teacher wanted to seem as if the work could be accomplished with no help at all.

Leader

"How can it be budget time again? They just signed off on the last one!" the principal muttered to himself. The current school committee was particularly challenging. There was one young guy who wanted to impress everyone with his smarts, and those twin sisters were impossible to persuade. The new superintendent wanted the public to like him, so he allowed the principals to make final budget cuts. Will Ford returned to poring over the spreadsheets. He was startled when his assistant buzzed and requested that he chat briefly with Ruby.

Ruby was stopping by with her weekly update on the novices. She had worked with Will Ford for years, and they liked and respected each other. Ruby trusted her principal enough to admit she was stymied, so she got right to the point.

"Will, I need your help. These young teachers are talented and well prepared, but not making progress. They don't even know what they don't know, but they don't seem to want help from me. We are two months in, and each one has dodged a meeting. I expected they'd want to collaborate on improving. I thought they might dive into the community together to learn all they could about where their children live. Instead, they spend so much effort on trying to look like everything is under control, and at the last bell, they jump into their cars and screech out of the parking lot headed in different directions. I try to take their perspective, but I'm confused. Don't they want mentoring? How can I gain their trust?"

Mr. Ford sat back in his chair. One of his goals was to reduce the turnover in the school, so here was an opportunity to work on teacher retention. Will also knew that he needed this challenge; the job of principal was all-consuming and all business. He'd hoped to be a teacher leader but over the years he'd assumed the role of district manager. He said to Ruby, "Let's cancel the working group and arrange the new teachers into a task force with the two of us taking the lead. We have some sticky problems to tackle this year. Maybe the group, with their fresh perspectives and our varied ideas and experiences, will come up with some answers."

"Let's start tomorrow," she replied.

Ruby did some of her best reflecting during her morning walk to school. As she crossed a historic footbridge, she paused to drop rocks she'd gathered into the quiet waters. Plop! She thought of Jack. He needed support on his behavior intervention plan. Splash! Ruby thought of Allie who loved the point of impact, but often neglected the circles spreading further and further from the original drop. And, of course, there was Rebecca, who wanted unwavering answers but needed to learn to flow like the river. That was, and is, the beauty and challenge of special education. There is never just one way. Ruby breathed deeply, taking in the pinkening sky. It was time to refresh the newbies in best practices and principles. She'd begin by reminding them that embracing the perspectives of others would be as important to them as to their students.

What do you think happens next?

Consider Ruby and her associates as you read the final chapters. Ruby and Will have embraced epistemic empathy, and they must now teach this skill to Rebecca, Jack, and Allie.

Novices enter the profession and old friends becoming veteran teachers will work together to tackle challenges. Social interaction and epistemic empathy will help them build a team that values input from the "knowledgeable other," a team that functions well because the perspectives of all are considered. What challenges will they face as they move forward? What is at stake for each participant? How will they work together to leverage talents and address weaknesses? How might this approach work for you?

CHAPTER 7

Collaboration

Collaboration is fundamental to special educators. Educating students with special needs relies on the contributions of many, from families to specialists to general educators. It is the role of the special educator to mediate this process, keeping the needs of the students at the forefront. Skills necessary for collaboration may be learned and practiced. Social interaction and epistemic empathy are vital to effective collaboration. Being able to work together on a shared goal is made easier when participants consider each other's perspectives. Communication is essential, and active listening contributes to successful communication. It is through collaboration among educators and families that students with disabilities will obtain the accommodations they need and transition to meaningful adult lives.

Teachers in special education become effective collaborators by developing interpersonal skills and learning how to make collaborative decisions to serve the needs of students with disabilities. While the previous chapter spotlighted social and emotional learning for students, this chapter presents these skills as they apply to adults collaborating. The skills include self-awareness, self-management, social awareness, relationship skills, and responsible decisionmaking.

Becoming an effective collaborator begins with developing *self-awareness* and *self-management*. Self-awareness is understanding how personal strengths, limitations, and emotions influence thinking. Self-management involves controlling one's own emotional reactions while absorbing new information.

RECOGNIZING THE PERSPECTIVE OF ANOTHER

Each of us sees the world through a personal lens. This view is shaped by experience, knowledge, environment, and so many other factors. Readiness to collaborate involves recognizing our own perspective (self-awareness) and welcoming the perspectives of others (self-management). Each collaborator interprets information differently (Lustig & Koester, 2013). Developing self-awareness and self-management for collaboration requires that the collaborator acknowledges his own viewpoint yet sincerely listens to the point of view of another. Epistemic empathy takes that listening one step further: Not only does the listener hear the perspective of another, but the listener is able to take that perspective.

Suggestions for Taking the Perspectives of Others

- Understand your personal perspective.
- Be aware of emotions that influence perspective.
- Acknowledge environmental factors, like hunger, fatigue, or stress.
- Avoid arriving at quick conclusions.
- Ask for clarification.
- Consider biases of both listener and speaker (adapted from Friend & Cook, 2017).

Cultural understanding also influences perspective. Teachers do well to understand their own cultural awareness and build their knowledge of other cultural perspectives. Acquisition of such information is part of social awareness, which involves learning social and ethical norms.

Suggestions for Building Cultural Perspective

- Articulate common ground.
- Explain cultural practices that are relevant.
- Show respect for cultural differences.
- Accept responsibility for your communication (adapted from Samovar et al., 2013).

The remaining social and emotional competencies as suggested by CASEL include social awareness, relationship building, and responsible decisionmaking. Relationship building is a significant precursor to effective collaboration.

DEVELOPING RELATIONSHIP SKILLS

Special educators collaborate with professionals, families, related service providers, individuals with disabilities, and community agencies.

ESSA, IDEA, and CEC Standards all address the importance of collaboration to support students with disabilities and their families.

Building relationships is the next social and emotional competency vital to collaboration. Being able to develop a team relies on communication, social engagement, and relationships. Effective relationships are the foundation for collaboration.

Suggestions for Building Relationship Skills

- Demonstrate empathy.
- Develop trust.
- Show interest.
- Promote acceptance.
- Listen actively.
- Exhibit sincerity.
- Balance communication.

Collaboration is a complex process. By its nature, it is voluntary; no one can be forced to collaborate. That's why relationship skills are fundamental. Even when assigned to teams, the team members will voluntarily decide the approach to problem solving. Will they follow a collaborative model, or will one person make the decisions? In collaboration, all team members' contributions have equal value. Roles and responsibilities are shared to carry out the decisions made in collaboration. As the decisions are being implemented, the collaborative team shares accountability for the outcomes.

Collaboration is also an emergent process. This means trust, respect, and the development of a sense of community may take time to develop (Friend, 2018).

FOSTERING RELATIONSHIP SKILLS AND TEACHING

Collaboration with all stakeholders is essential for special educators. General education teachers, teacher assistants, administrators, families, students are all part of the fabric of the day for a special educator. However, at the instructional level, relationship skills impact co-teaching. Co-teaching is a service delivery model that has been used to support students with disabilities. Paired co-teachers may include a general and a special education teacher, or a teacher and a related service professional, or a teacher and another specialist (Friend

& Cook, 2017). The goal is to combine their expertise to jointly teach a heterogeneous group of students, some with disabilities or special needs (Friend, 2018).

The goal in co-teaching is to maximize the expertise of both individuals (Dieker & Rodriguez, 2013; Murawski, 2015). To set the stage for effective co-teaching, the two professionals need to clearly communicate with each other—instructional philosophies, strengths and weaknesses, and expectations for both co-teachers. This conversation will prepare the two professionals for co-teaching and for determining how to best use their talents in a co-teaching setting (Friend, 2018).

Friend (2014) presented six co-teaching models:

One teach; one observe. This model is when one teacher is teaching the entire group and the second teacher is collecting data on one student, a small group of students, or the entire class. An example of this model is when a co-teacher collects data for RTI on social interactions during small-group work.

Parallel teaching. This model is when the two teachers split the large group and each teaches the same content. An example of this model is a review session where the smaller groups can receive more attention and answers to individual questions.

Station teaching. Here the instruction is provided in two, three, four or more individual settings. Students work on nonsequential activities guided by one of the co-teachers, and there may also be independent stations for self-guided work.

Alternative teaching. This is when one of the co-teachers pulls aside a small group of students for different instruction. This may happen through pre-teaching, additional guided practice, or enrichment activities.

Teaming. This approach is when the two co-teachers fluidly share the instructional responsibilities; for example, one teacher provides a whole-class minilesson while the other teacher writes key vocabulary on the board and asks meaningful questions to guide student learning.

One teach; one assist. One teacher provides whole-class instruction while the other teacher may support individual students during this instruction. Either teacher may take either role in this setting.

ENHANCING SOCIAL AWARENESS AND COMMUNICATION

Communication skills are essential for effective collaboration. Communication must be both effective and appropriate (Martin & Nakayama, 2015). Effective communication demands *social awareness*, the fourth skill as recognized by CASEL.

Communication is impacted by social, emotional, physical, and cognitive factors. Knowing how these factors affect the person with whom the communication is taking place is social awareness.

To have effective and appropriate communication, a special educator develops skills in the following three communication areas. First, there is professional and ethical communication. All communication should stem from the foundation of respect, honesty, and cultural understanding. It should be mutual and shared. Next is awareness of nonverbal behaviors, which signal attention (or its lack) and communicate reactions through gesture, eye contact, and body position. The third area is responding skills. These are when one paraphrases, prompts, uses open-ended questions, and reflects (Friend & Cook, 2017).

Suggestions for Practicing Social Awareness When Communicating

- Demonstrate active listening by repeating what you just heard.
- Provide positive reactions through verbal and nonverbal avenues.
- Be present, not distracted by technology or time.
- Do not interrupt.
- Remember one can listen faster than one can speak (Friend, 2018).

Collaboration in schools. A collaborative school culture, supported by strong guiding leadership, has shown positive achievement outcomes for students with disabilities (Huberman et al., 2012). Students' proficiency in reading and math improved significantly in school districts emphasizing collaborative, shared leadership. The collaborative culture included common planning time, co-teaching, and teaming (Silverman et al., 2009).

Shannon and Blysma (2007) conducted an overview of research on successful schools. Of the characteristics that emerged from the research that described successful results-oriented schools, one was that high levels of collaboration and communication were essential. Successful schools had effective communication that was high-quality and timely among team members. Staff focused on things that mattered: curriculum and instruction, improving practice, and student success. There was a strong sense of community; not only school staff, but community members and families were engaged in the educational decisionmaking process. For collaboration and communication to be impactful, schools provided time, support, and a structure for collaboration. Teams reflected the diversity of the school and broader community. Multiple means of communication were used from electronic communications to home visits. Caron and McLaughlin (2002) found that schools that showed student growth had collaborative planning, co-teaching opportunities, strong school leadership, trust among team members, high expectations for all learners, and a sense of a professional school community.

A form of collaboration specific to special educators is the intense work done with teaching assistants. Their shared goal is to promote social-emotional and academic growth of students with disabilities; however, each has a different role. Thorough explanation and understanding of the roles leads to better collaboration. This requires a plan (Carnahan et al., 2009). An effective plan entails communication based on a shared philosophy (Giangreco et al., 2003). Clear expectations are essential. The teaching assistant's responsibilities are guided and supervised by the qualified special educator, who relies heavily on the TA's expertise. The special educator sets the tone for this working relationship, and when the tone is one of respect, the students will benefit.

Suggestions for Working with Teaching Assistants

- Welcome and initiate the TA to the team.
- Employ epistemic empathy when communicating.
- Get to know each other's strengths and challenges.
- Elicit input from the TA regarding instructional decisions.
- Plan together when possible.
- Provide the TA with concrete suggestions and directions.
- Jointly articulate the parameters for working with students.
- Provide the TA with meaningful work including data collection, small group instruction, and assessment.
- Incorporate the TA's ideas regarding the organization of resources.

Collaboration with families. To build collaboration with families, a special educator must begin with a clear understanding that every family is unique and influenced by factors such as ethnicity, language, socioeconomic status, and family structure (Hagiwara & Shogren, 2019). Developing collaborative partnerships between school professionals and families depends on effective communication, professional competence, respect, commitment, equality, advocacy, and trust (Turnbull et al., 2015). The relationship is reciprocal—both parties have information to share. Teachers need to clearly understand family strengths and goals for their children (Hagiwara & Shogren, 2019). This forms the bridge for collaborative communication.

Collaborative relationships with families are emergent. They take time to develop. Frequent and meaningful communication is necessary. Building trust among school personnel and families is based on establishing a sense of belonging and commitment. This collaboration will ultimately lead to quality education and quality of life for professionals, families, and students (Blue-Banning et al., 2004).

Suggestions for Communicating with Families

- Survey parents for preferred mode of communication.
- Communicate frequently with brief messages (Kraft, 2017).
- Focus on strengths during parent meetings.
- Reflect family's culture in the classroom.
- Welcome and value all families (Minkel, 2017).
- Engage in the community outside of school.
- Treat parents with kindness and respect (Goodwin, 2017).
- Respond promptly to concerns.

Another way to foster collaboration between school and families is through establishing roles for families in school operations. This includes making opportunities for families to participate in school governance, developing leadership roles for families, and supporting new families by providing leadership opportunities to all (Francis et al., 2016).

Responsible decisionmaking. This is the final social and emotional competency applicable to collaboration. Problems are identified and analyzed. Once a problem is solved, the solution is evaluated through reflection. To make decisions, a problem-solving structure is needed. This structure is based on effective communication and will lead to accomplishing a common goal in a collaborative manner. In the next chapter we provide a problem-solving structure with its roots in epistemic empathy.

EPISTEMIC EMPATHY EXERCISE

Ruby slammed the papers down on the desk and marched out the door in a huff. Ruby was furious at the way the general education teacher, Ms. Michaud, was treating not only her, but the students in the room who needed special education. Again, this morning, Ruby had felt diminished as the classroom teacher barked instructions. "Please take the kids who aren't following the lesson to the table at the back of the room. You can do some review work there while the rest of us move on to decimals." This was not what Ruby had expected.

The promise of inclusion guided every decision Ruby made for students with special needs. Not only was it the law, but she knew it was the right thing to do. She wanted all the students in her case-load to actualize their potential—to participate fully as adults in their community. She assumed the general education teacher assigned to the inclusion classroom agreed, but it was increasingly evident that inclusion meant something very different to the two professionals in the room.

The general education teacher sent Ms. Rok a quick text, "She's mad again! I can't do anything right!" Ms. Rok and the general educator were best friends, and Ms. Rok had been trying to be supportive as her old pal, Ms. Michaud, suffered through an excruciating divorce. However, she knew that the conflict in the classroom was impacting the students. Ms. Rok reached out to Mr. Ford for advice. What do you think happened next?

BRIDGE BUILDER

The graphic organizer below will help you structure your discussion of the issue presented in the Epistemic Empathy Exercise. In the left column are listed the persons involved in the dilemma. Respond to the questions in the right column as the designated person would respond. Use epistemic empathy; take the perspective of another in order to analyze the issue. Collaborate to solve the problem.

Ruby	How will Mr. Ford feel when he hears about the tension with Ms. Michaud? How will Ms. Rok strategize a solution when the conflict is between her best friend and me?
Mr. Ford	Why can't Ruby and Ms. Michaud work this out? How is Ms. Rok handling this situation between her best friend and Ruby?
Ms. Rok	Why is Ruby having such a difficult time getting along with my friend? How will Mr. Ford feel when he sees two of his teachers in conflict?
Collaborative Solution	How can we *build* the relationship between Ruby and Ms. Michaud? Let's *determine* some norms the teachers can adopt to continue to collaborate.

CHAPTER 8

Application

Mentor

Allie stood gazing at the night sky from the window overlooking her garden. Sleep had eluded her since she'd heard the news. Someone had set fire to the shed containing the athletic equipment for the district. The crisis was over, but Allie knew the aftershocks might be just as devastating. On social media, citizen and parent groups were targeting students with emotional and behavior disorders as potential arsonists. Talk radio was blaring accusations, targeting students with autism, depression, and ADHD as well as English learners, kids from poverty and nontraditional homes. It was time to inform, to model, to teach, and to advocate. Allie and the team would hush the hysteria and protect the children.

She began to plan. Her first step would be to work with the new teachers under her wing. She thought back to her first years of teaching, and how Ruby brought out the best in her and in Jack and Rebecca. Allie knew that her own charges were enthusiastic and committed to the students. She looked forward to talking with Tom, a first-year teacher who grew up in the community and would shed light on the best ways to steady the ship. Tom and her other mentees had needed help throughout the semester, and Allie had loved supporting them. She knew that Tom would provide valuable insights in this endeavor, and she knew she'd be learning from him. Her thoughts drifted back to her own first year of teaching and, she wondered with a smile, if perhaps Ruby had learned something from her.

In the still of the night, she began to brainstorm. They'd need to work with families, meet with the general education faculty, develop materials for outreach. Research needed to be done—how had other communities responded? What did the national organization have to contribute to this dilemma? As the sky turned pale pink, Allie stretched and went into the kitchen to turn on the coffee.

Novice

Tom crashed at his parents' home early Saturday morning, carrying his laundry and a bag of doughnuts for the family. He slumped into his old kitchen chair and dropped his head onto the familiar table. His mom and dad, retired social workers, were seated at the table having their oatmeal and doing the crossword puzzle together. They stared in shock at their crestfallen son.

"Honey? Are you all right?" his mom gently asked.

Tom banged a fist on the table.

"Didn't you hear? Someone burned down a school building. It was probably one of my kids! They're saying it was a kid with an IEP," growled the novice teacher.

His parents stiffened. His dad's eyes filled with tears. At that very moment, Tom's 25-year-old brother bounced into the kitchen. As a person on the autism spectrum, he could get fixated on an activity.

"I reached the next level," he announced, waving his tablet in the air.

Tom froze.

"Sorry, Mom and Dad," he whispered. "I should know better than anyone." He repeated the family mantra: "Innocent until proven guilty. Stereotyping doesn't help. We just need to help others understand."

Tom's phone buzzed. He looked down to read the text from his mentor, Allie. It said, "T. We need to brainstorm. We need to advocate for the kids. Time to plan?"

Tom texted back. "I'm in."

Ruby Thrives as Leader

As the Director of Special Education, Ruby was responsible for organizing professional development offerings for the academic year. It was a responsibility she took very seriously, and today was the day she'd make final decisions. She shuffled once more through the brochures and letters the administrative assistant had kept for her perusal and looked again at the lists she'd made. Certainly, there were excellent offerings, but she knew this year had to be different.

In the wake of the fire, Ruby had received 62 phone calls from the press, parents, other members of the district. Clearly, people were looking to assign blame for the incident. They couldn't bear to think that some typical student had caused such mayhem. But, as a member of the leadership team, Ruby had inside information, and she knew that was indeed the case. A student had procured gasoline and lighter fluid from the nearby hardware store. The student was an above-average student from an apparently healthy family. He had friends and interests. The truth was there had been no warning signs.

The op-ed page was filled with letters to the editor, suggesting that the perpetrator would be found to be a student with an emotional/behavioral disorder. Ruby was devastated by this. She needed people to stop this trend in its tracks. Ruby recognized that workshops and presentations wouldn't lead to the sea-change she sought. She'd need a creative, far-reaching response. How best to leverage faculty, staff, students, and families to challenge assumptions about students with special needs? It was time to build a bridge.

LEVERAGING SOCIAL INTERACTION, EPISTEMIC EMPATHY, AND DISCIPLINARY KNOWLEDGE

The readers of this book, from those just completing teacher preparation programs to veterans in the field, have found familiar material on these pages. But the information has been presented from a new perspective. Emphasis has been on the power of epistemic empathy across the profession—from its value as a teaching tool to its power for succession planning. On these final pages, it is presented in action as part of a problem-solving process. The BRIDGE model engages participants in steps toward problem solving. It is built on elements resonant of a bridge: coming at situations from two sides, meeting in the middle, viewing an issue from two perspectives. Some familiar characters will employ the BRIDGE model to solve a problematic situation by activating epistemic empathy. In fact, the steps will also have a ring of familiarity. You will have been using them as you completed the Bridge Builders.

BRIDGE: A PROBLEM-SOLVING MODEL

The BRIDGE problem-solving model is unique in that the emphasis is on the solvers rather than on the problem. The model is built on several assumptions:

- Solutions to problems frequently exist.
- Professionals in the field have the knowledge, skills, and experience to find solutions.

- Collaboration contributes to a problem-solving team's effectiveness.
- The process for finding solutions is effective when epistemic empathy and social interaction are at its foundation, all members are heard, and members truly listen to perspectives of others.

Steps for integrating collaboration at the outset of a problem-solving process are listed below. We introduce you to the BRIDGE.

Build the team. Relationships contribute to the functioning of a team. However, the roles of novice, mentor, and leader come loaded with assumptions that often block good communication. For the team to benefit from the experiences and perspectives of all members, it's important to recognize that any contributor may serve as the "knowledgeable other" in some circumstances. A preliminary step will include that the team articulate and acknowledge epistemic empathy. Strong foundational relationships will contribute to the effectiveness of problem solving.

Review the problem together. So much of the success of this approach depends on relationship-building and communication, which rely on social interaction and epistemic empathy. Prioritize understanding the other's perspective. Discuss the problem in all its complexity. Each participant will provide a unique perspective. Gather them all. Ensure a safe environment for sharing thinking. Again, it's imperative that each member—novice, mentor, and leader—be considered a valuable resource.

Investigate the possibilities. Once the problem is articulated with common language in the previous step, it is time to sort, choose, and designate tasks. Because epistemic empathy and social interaction guide the process, all ideas are possible and should be considered. The team works together to narrow the possible solutions, and assignments are made to team members, individually or together, to investigate the options. Once the goal is established, a timeline is needed. Benchmarks and interim steps must be delineated. Personal strengths and weaknesses are considered, but work is shared. The plan becomes the shared focus. The plan also has clear criteria for measuring progress and solution to the problem.

**D**etermine the best solution. Nothing is more precious than time. Nothing is more disheartening than wasting that commodity.

Discussion of possible solutions is the next step. Articulation of how success will be measured is critical at this step. Participating in a group where epistemic empathy is employed does not guarantee unanimity; rather, it promises that all contributions will be valued. When all members have been heard, when respectful discussion has occurred, the problem-solvers choose a direction.

**G**et going! The next part of the process is where progress can be charted. It is usually a spiral in that, although work may be dispersed, all parties gear toward benchmarks and interim goals, convene, and revisit the problem. The group moves forward, but constantly revisits the work that has been completed, the progress that has been made, the lessons that have been learned. The group is also always calibrating its next steps, looking ahead toward the solution and considering ways in which the work will be different from what was expected. As such, the path from beginning to completion is not a straight line but a spiral. This spiraling format will provide many opportunities for those involved to learn about the thinking process of the others. It is in this work where novices deepen their roots, leaders recognize change, and future leaders may be coached.

**E**valuate outcomes. Because the group has previously decided how success will be measured, this step may seem straightforward. Has the problem been solved? Is there further work to accomplish? In addition, the effort must be evaluated. Did working with this process deepen each participant's understanding of the roles and perspectives of others? What broader skills were gained? How have the participants changed?

BRIDGE: IN ACTION

The BRIDGE process relies on participants, at various points in their careers, hearing and respecting their colleagues' insights and needs. Read on to examine how the BRIDGE process scaffolds conversation and problem-solving by building bridges among professionals.

**B**uild the team. Tom, Allie, and Ruby had a strong bond. As professionals in special education, they had discussed the importance of perception. Historically, progress had been made in some areas. People with disabilities were no longer sequestered in institutional settings, and they were often participants in the community. But was there true inclusion? The participation of those with disabilities was often sidelined or sporadic. And when funds were short in school systems, they were often blamed: out-of-district placements, special transportation, extra teaching assistants. To provide free and appropriate education for those with needs had a cost. The threesome talked about their own experiences. Allie's years in the field had shown her that attitudes were contagious, and that teaching about persons with disabilities demystified them for others. Tom felt anger, first at public opinion, and then at himself for being swayed by public opinion. He was passionate in his need to right this wrong. Ruby, who had the larger picture, knew the group needed to be deliberate. Time sometimes lessened passions, and it sometimes fueled them. They'd have to get a better feel for the environment.

Review the problem together. Together they discussed the problem and articulated a goal. They'd need a public relations response to this situation. They brainstormed, furiously writing all thoughts on the whiteboards that covered the walls of the meeting room. Who needed to hear the response? Where? How? Should students be involved? They tried to take the perspectives of others. What needed to be addressed for each group of stakeholders? The conversation was fast-paced and filled with emotion, but after several hours, they looked at all they'd written, and knew they had developed a broad understanding of the issue they faced.

Investigate the possibilities. An important step was to be sure they shared a common goal. Each wrote an idea for solving the problem on a slip of paper. The differences were startling. Allie wrote, "Develop a presentation for the public that shows what we do in special education." Tom's stated goal was, "Ensure that students with special needs do not become targets of negative stereotyping." Ruby, carefully considering her new position, wrote, "Articulate a plan for sharing success stories of students receiving special education services." It was clear they'd need to collaborate so that multiple perspectives were represented in the goal they'd pursue. Ultimately, the shared goal was written as, "Establish and present a multi-tiered information program to foster positive attitudes toward students with special needs and their educational programs." Now they'd need to investigate possible ways for meeting that goal. They determined that success would mean that an appeal to the school committee for funds to develop such a program would be met with approval.

Determine the best solution. Allie, Ruby, and Tom next considered the best avenue for moving forward. The trio decided to present to the school committee, in graphic detail, what services were being provided and outcomes of students receiving services. In addition, they'd invite students with special needs and their families to share stories.

Get going! Between gathering and organizing the data, developing the presentation, and practicing, the task took a month. But, by the quarterly school committee meeting, they were ready. Their presentation ended with a list of action steps to follow up on their opening salvo.

Evaluate the outcome. The response from the school committee was positive, and the team received funding for moving ahead. They'd use this problem-solving method to address each tier of the program. They'd invite others to join the efforts to build awareness of just how special education worked. In the process, they learned to think about issues from a variety of perspectives.

As Tom headed home after the school committee presentation, he thought to himself, "I think I'd like to be Director of Special Education one day."

Now it's your turn. Engage as a team using epistemic empathy, social interaction, and the BRIDGE model to solve the problem presented below.

EPISTEMIC EMPATHY EXERCISE

Final Challenge

The principal, Ms. Richard, has asked for volunteers to help with a difficult situation. The newest member of the team, a special educator, is ready to work with the team to address the problem.

Mr. Pimental, a member of the school committee, has made the following statement:

> We keep hearing about a shortage of special educators; it
> has become clear that many positions will go unfilled. At the

same time, my niece, a recent grad of the local university's education program, can't get a job! What's the disconnect here? Why aren't we filling teaching positions in special education? I believe it's a ploy by organized labor to force us to raise salaries. Good teaching is good teaching! I think it is time to get rid of specialized certifications and open up the opportunities to all.

Discuss the importance and use of epistemic empathy to effectively dialogue with the politician and all stakeholders. What can you discover about the perspectives of others?

Discuss how you would use the BRIDGE process to solve the problem.

Build the team
Review the problem together
Investigate the possibilities
Determine the best solution
Get going
Evaluate the outcome

BRIDGE BUILDER

The graphic organizer below will help you structure your discussion of the issue presented in the Epistemic Empathy Exercise. In the left column are listed the persons involved in the dilemma. Respond to the questions in the right column as the designated person would respond. Use epistemic empathy; take the perspective of another in order to analyze the issue. Collaborate using the BRIDGE process to solve the problem.

Ms. Richard (Principal)	How can I possibly talk to my special educators about this idea? What is Mr. Pimental's background to be suggesting this?
Mr. Pimental (School Committee Member)	Why doesn't Ms. Richard see the practicality of this solution? How can I get the support of the principal and special education teachers?
Special Educator (Novice)	Why does Ms. Richard think a person could do my position without the proper training? Why doesn't Mr. Pimental value my role as a special educator?
Collaborative Solution	Build the team Review the problem together Investigate the possibilities Determine the best solution Get going Evaluate the outcome

THE PROVIDENCE PEDESTRIAN BRIDGE

The Providence Pedestrian Bridge serves as our final offering. The image reveals a silent, forlorn place. In reality, it will soon become a hub of activity. The Providence Pedestrian Bridge signifies the power of possibility. The space has great potential; change is coming to the bridge.

In the pages of this book, the reader has been presented with the possibility of an empowering way of living in the world of special education—empowering for students, empowering for families, and empowering for professionals in the field. Attention has been paid to the discipline's basic principles and best practices. Acknowledgment has been given to the importance of professional development and social interaction. These important components of special education are enhanced when all stakeholders embrace epistemic empathy.

The Providence Pedestrian Bridge curves to meet the needs of the landscape, a design echoic of special education. As pedestrians cross the bridge, their perspectives change as they follow the bends in the path. Epistemic empathy works much the same way. By taking the perspective of each student, a special educator designs instruction that is most effective for that individual. By taking the perspectives of colleagues and supervisors, professionals in special education learn to see the horizon from varied points of view.

The Providence Pedestrian Bridge is the culminating span building on earlier comparisons. Pictures of additional bridges were provided to emphasize important ideas. The metaphor began with the image of the Brooklyn Bridge, a bastion of stability. That bridge initiated the reader with its reminder of how invaluable a strong foundation is. The photo to follow captured the startling adaptability of the Rolling Bridge. The architects of the Rolling Bridge created a solid structure of amazing versatility. The image of this unique work reinforced the value of flexibility. Like a good special educator, the Rolling Bridge adapts for those who need it.

Third, the Mostar Bridge, a breathtaking span, was chosen to exemplify the value of collaboration. The Mostar was built to replace a historic structure that had been damaged during war. The photo of the glorious Mostar was included because its significance comes from its development. Various countries and agencies moved forward with one purpose, to build the bridge. When educators collaborate with one purpose, to actualize the potential of students with special needs, bridge building is possible.

And, Ruby, whose story is traced throughout the book, personifies the values represented by the bridges. The reader is given a birds-eye view as Ruby brings to life the theories and best practices presented. She journeys forward, crossing each new bridge, always trying, always learning, always improving. It is for teachers like Ruby that we end with the Providence Pedestrian Bridge. Before the morning sun reaches its peak over Providence, the quiet span will become a meeting place. People with varied perspectives will share ideas, stories, and laughter as they come together on the bridge. The structure provides choices. Some walkers may pause to reflect and gaze at the running river. Others will engage fellow pedestrians in games of chess on the boards set up along the way. Many will enter the space with one destination in mind and will change course completely upon encountering a friend. Most travelers will cross the bridge from where they are to where they want to be, a journey also taken by those who employ the BRIDGE problem-solving model provided in the last chapter.

Growing as a special educator requires a passage much like crossing the Providence Pedestrian Bridge. We stop to reflect; we undertake challenges; we collaborate to solve problems. When we do all of these with epistemic empathy, when we see the world through the eyes of another, the view becomes much wider, much more inclusive. And that, after all, is the purpose of special education.

References

Agoratus, L. (2016). The effects of ESSA (Every Student Succeeds Act) for children with disabilities. *Exceptional Parent, 46*(9), 26–27.

Ainsworth, L. (2003). *"Unwrapping" the standards: A simple process to make standards manageable.* Lead + Learn Press.

Alber-Morgan, S. R., Helton, M. R., Telesman, A. O., & Konrad, M. (2019). Adapt curriculum tasks and materials for specific learning goals. In J. McLeskey, L. Maheady, B. Billingsley, M. T. Brownell, & T. J. Lewis (Eds.), *High leverage practices for inclusive classrooms* (pp. 170–180). Routledge.

Alber-Morgan, S. R., Konrad, M., Hessler, T., Helton, M. R., & Telesman, A. O. (2019). Identify and prioritize long- and short-term learning goals. In J. McLeskey, L. Maheady, B. Billingsley, M. T. Brownell, & T. J. Lewis (Eds.), *High leverage practices for inclusive classrooms* (pp. 145–156). Routledge.

Alberto, P., & Troutman, A. (2013). *Applied behavioral analysis for teachers* (9th ed.). Pearson.

Almond, P. J., & Case, B. J. (2004). *Alternative assessments for students with significant cognitive disabilities.* Pearson.

Alper, S., & Raharinirina, S. (2006). Assistive technology for individuals with disabilities: A review and synthesis of the literature. *Journal of Special Education and Technology, 21*(2), 47–64.

Baptiste, N., & Sheerer, M. (1997). Negotiating the challenges of the "Survival" stage of professional development. *Early Childhood Education Journal, 24*(4), 265–267.

Bartlett, L. D., Etscheidt, S., & Weisenstein, G. R. (2007). *Special education law and practice in public schools* (2nd ed.). Merrill/Pearson Education.

Blue-Banning, M., Summers, J. A., Frankland, H. C., Nelson, L. L., & Beegle, G. (2004). Dimensions of family and professional partnerships: Constructive guidelines for collaboration. *Exceptional Children, 70*(2), 167–184.

Bouton, B. (2016). Empathy research and teacher preparation: Benefits and obstacles. *SRATE Journal, 25*(2), 16–25.

Boykin, A. W, & Noguera, P. (2011). *Creating the opportunity to learn: Moving from research to practice to close the achievement gap.* Association for Supervision and Curriculum Development.

Breiseth, L. (2016). Getting to know ELLs' families. *Educational Leadership, 72*(5), 46–50.

Brown, M. R. (2007). Educating all students: Creating Culturally Responsive teachers, classrooms and schools. *Intervention in School & Clinic, 33*(1), 57–62.

Brownell, M. T. (2019). Assessment high leverage practices. In J. McLeskey, L. Maheady, B. Billingsley, M. T. Brownell, & T. J. Lewis (Eds.), *High leverage practices for inclusive classrooms* (pp. 49–50). Routledge.

Bunting, C. (2007, January). Teachers get personal about teaching to survive NCLB. *Education Digest, 72*(5), 12–15.

Byrnes, M. (2000, February). Accommodations for students with disabilities: Removing barriers to learning. *NASSP Bulletin*, 21–27.

Carnahan, C. R., Williamson, P., Clarke, L., & Sorenson, R. (2009). A systematic approach for supporting paraeducators in educational settings: A guide for teachers. *Teaching Exceptional Children, 41*(5), 34–43.

Caron, E. A., & McLaughlin, M. J. (2002). Indicators of beacons of excellence schools: What do they tell us about collaborative practice? *Journal of Educational and Psychological Consultation, 13*(4), 285.

Center for Parent Information and Resources (2018, April 3). *Amendments to IDEA made by ESSA*. www.parentcenterhub.org/amends-to-idea-essa-fact-sheet/

Cesar, M., & Santos, N. (2006) From exclusion to inclusion: Collaborative work contributions to more inclusive learning setting. *European Journal of Psychology of Education, 21*(3), 333–346.

Chen, G. (2019, October 14). White students are now the minority in U.S. public schools. *Public School Review*. https://www.publicschoolreview.com/blog/white-students-are-now-the-minority-in-u-s-public-schools

Chou, H. (2007). Multicultural teacher education: Toward a culturally responsible pedagogy. *Essays in Education, 21*, 139–162.

Coleman, D., & Pimentel, S. (2012a). *Revised publishers' criteria for the common core state standards in English language arts and literacy, grades K–2*. Core Standards. www.corestandards.org/assets/Publishers_Criteria_for_K-2.pdf

Coleman, D., & Pimentel, S. (2012b). *Revised publishers' criteria for the common core state standards in English language arts and literacy, grades 3–12*. Core Standards. www.corestandards.org/assets/Publishers_Criteria_for_3-12.pdf

Collaborative for Academic, Social, and Emotional Learning (CASEL). (2020, April 22). *What is SEL?* https://casel.org/what-is-sel/

Common Core State Standards–Mathematics (2012, July 20). *K–8 publishers' criteria for the common core state standards for mathematics*. Core Standards. www.corestandards.org/assets/Math_Publishers_Criteri a_K-8_Summer%202012_FINAL.pdf

Cooper, B. (2004, September). Empathy, interaction and caring: Teachers' roles in a constrained environment. *Pastoral Care*, 12–21.

Coster, W., Law, M., Bedell, G., Liljenquist, K., Kao, Y. C., Khetani, M., & Teplicky, R. (2013). School participation, supports and barriers of students with and without disabilities. *Childcare, Health and Development, 39*(4), 535–543.

Council for Exceptional Children & CEEDAR Center (2017). *High leverage practices in special education*. highleveragepractices.org

Craig, S. E. (2016) The trauma-sensitive teacher. *Educational Leadership, 74*(1), 28–32.

Cummins, J. (2008) BICS and CALP: Empirical and theoretical status of the distinction. In B. Street & N. H. Hornberger (Eds.), *Encyclopedia of Language and Education, 2nd Edition, Volume 2: Literacy* (pp. 71–83). Springer Science + Business Media LLC.

Deady, K. (2017). *5 steps to becoming a culturally responsive teacher*. Teachaway. www.teachaway.com/blog/5-steps-becoming-culturally-responsive-teacher

Dieker, L. A., & Rodriguez, J. A. (2013). Enhancing secondary co-taught science and mathematics classrooms through collaboration. *Intervention in School & Clinic, 49*(1), 46–53.

Dillon, R. (2018) Room for improvement: Becoming more intentional about classroom design can help teachers manage behavior, build community and improve learning. *Educational Leadership, (76)*1, 40–45.

Doabler, C. T., Nelson, N. J., & Clarke, B. (2016). Adapting evidence-based practices to meet the needs of English learners with mathematics difficulties. *Teaching Exceptional Children, 48*(6), 301–310. doi.org/10.1177/0040059916650638

Ellerbrock, C. R., Abbas, B., Diciccio, M., Denmon, J. M., Sabella, L., & Hart, J. (2015). Relationships: The fundamental R in Education. *Phi Delta Kappan, 96*(8), 48–51.

Erickson, R., Ysseldyke, J., Thurlow, M., & Elliott, J. (1998). Inclusive assessments and accountability systems. *Teaching Exceptional Children, 31*(2), 4–9.

Evertson, C. M., & Emmer, E. T. (2017). *Classroom management for elementary teachers* (10th ed.). Pearson.

Field, S. L., & Hoffman, A. S. (2012). Fostering self-determination through building productive relationships on the classroom. *Intervention in School and Clinic, 48*(1), 6–14. doi.org/10.1177/1053451212443150

Fisher, A. V., Godwin, K. E., & Seltman, H. (2014). Visual environment, attention allocation, and learning in young children: When too much of a good thing may be bad. *Psychological Science, (25)*7, 1362–1370.

Francis, G. L., Blue-Banning, M., Haines, S. J., Turnbull, A. P., & Gross, J. M. S. (2016). Building "our school": Parental perspectives for building trusting family-professional partnerships. *Preventing School Failure, 60*(4), 329–336.

Frey, N., Fisher, D., & Smith, D. (2019). *All learning is social and emotional: Helping students develop essential skills for the classroom and beyond.* ASCD Publications.

Friend, M. (2014). *Co-teach! A handbook for creating and sustaining effective classroom partnerships in inclusive schools* (2nd ed.). Marilyn Friend, Inc.

Friend, M. (2018). *Special education contemporary perspectives for school professionals* (5th ed.). Pearson.

Friend, M., & Bursuck, W. D. (2019). *Including students with special needs: A practical guide for classroom teachers* (8th ed.). Pearson.

Friend, M., & Cook, L. (2017). *Interactions: Collaboration skills for school professionals* (8th ed.). Pearson.

Gallimore, R., & Tharp, R. G. (1990). Teaching mind in society: Teaching, schooling and literate discourse. In L. C. Moll (Ed.), *Vygotsky and education: Instructional implications and applications of sociohistorical psychology* (pp. 175–206). Cambridge University Press.

Gallucci, C. (2008). Districtwide instructional reform: Using sociocultural theory to link professional learning to organizational support. *American Journal of Education, 114*(4), 541–548.

Gargiulo, R. M., & Metcalf, D. (2010). *Teaching in today's inclusive classroom: A universal design for learning approach.* Wadsworth CENGAGE Learning.

Giangreco, M. F., Backus, L., CichoskiKelly, E., Sherman, P., & Mavropoulos, Y. (2003). Paraeducator training materials to facilitate inclusive education: Initial field-test data. *Rural Special Education Quarterly, 22*(1), 17–27.

Glover, T. A., & Vaughn, S. (2010). *The promise of response to intervention: Evaluating current science and practice.* Guilford.

Gomez, M. L. (1994). Teacher education reform and prospective teachers' perspectives on teaching "other people's" children. *Teaching and Teacher Education, 10*(3), 319–334.

Goodman, G., Bains, L., & Moussalli, M. (2011). IEP workboxes: An intervention for increasing the cognitive development of preschool students with disabilities. *Intervention in School and Clinic, 46*, 251–256. doi.org/10.1177/1053451210389037

Goodwin, B. (2017). The power of parental expectations. *Educational Leadership, 75*(1), 80–81.

Gresham, F. M. (2004). Current status and future directions of school-based behavioral interventions. *School Psychology Review, 33*(3), 326–343.

Griner, A. C., & Stewart, M. L. (2013). Addressing the achievement gap and disproportionality through the use of culturally responsive teaching practices. *Urban Education, 48*(4), 585–621. doi.org/10.1177/0042085912456847

Hagiwara, M., & Shogren, K. A. (2019). Collaborate with families to support student learning and secure needed services. In J. McLeskey, L, Maheady, B. Billingsley, M. T. Brownell, & T. J. Lewis (Eds.), *High leverage practices for inclusive classrooms* (pp. 34–47). Routledge.

Hattie, J. (2008). *Visible learning: A synthesis of over 800 meta-analyses relating to achievement.* Routledge.

Henderson, N. (2013). Havens of resilience. *Educational Leadership, 71*(1), 22–27.

Heward, W. L. (2019). Use strategies to promote active student engagement. In J. McLeskey, L. Maheady, B. Billingsley, M. T. Brownell, & T. J. Lewis (Eds.), *High leverage practices for inclusive classrooms* (pp. 251–263). Routledge.

Hirsch, S., Bruhn, A. L., Lloyd, J. W., & Katsiyannis, A. (2017). FBAs and BIPs: Avoiding and addressing four common challenges related to fidelity. *Teaching Exceptional Children, 49*(6), 369–379.

Hodgkinson, H. (2002). Demographics and teacher education: An overview. *Journal of Teacher Education, 52*(2), 102–105.

Hoffman, J. (2002). Flexible grouping strategies in the multiage classroom. *Theory into Practice, 41*(1), 47–52.

Horner, R. H., Sugai, G., & Anderson, C. M. (2010). Examining the evidence base for schoolwide positive behavior support. *Focus on Exceptional Children, 42*(8), 1–14.

Howard, G. (2007). As diversity grows, so must we. *Educational Leadership, 64*(6), 16–22.

Howard, G. R. (2012, September 13). *Seven principles of culturally responsive teaching and learning* [video]. https://www.youtube.com/watch?v=IptefRjN4DY

Huberman, M., Navo, M., & Parrish, T. (2012). Effective practices in high performing districts serving students in special education. *Journal of Special Education Leadership, 25*(2), 59–71.

Hughes, C. (2011). Effective instructional design and delivery for teaching task-specific learning strategies to students with learning disabilities. *Focus on Exceptional Children, 44*(2), 1–16.

Hughes, C. A., Riccomini, P. J., & Morris, J. R. (2019). Use explicit instruction. In J. McLeskey, L. Maheady, B. Billingsley, M. T. Brownell, & T. J. Lewis (Eds.), *High leverage practices for inclusive classrooms* (pp. 215–236). Routledge.

Hussar, W., & Bailey, T. M. (2018, April). *Projections for Education Statistics to 2026.* U.S. Department of Education. https://nces.ed.gov/pubs2018/2018019.pdf

Jackson, S. (1948, June 26). The lottery. *The New Yorker.* https://www.newyorker.com/magazine/1948/06/26/the-lottery

Janney, R., & Snell, M. E. (2000). *Behavioral support.* Brookes.

Jones, S. M., Bailey, R., Brion-Meisels, G., & Partee, A. (2016). Choosing to be positive. *Educational Leadership, 74*(1), 63–68.

Kennedy, M. (2017, May/June). Seat yourself: Providing students a variety of seating choices in a classroom helps enhance learning opportunities. *American School & University, 89*(8), 26–28.

Konrad, M., Hessler, T., Alber-Morgan, S. R., Davenport, C. A., & Helton, M. R. (2019). Systematically design instruction toward a specific goal. In J. McLeskey, L. Maheady, B. Billingsley, M. T. Brownell, & T. J. Lewis (Eds.), *High leverage practices for inclusive classrooms* (pp. 157–169). Routledge.

Kraft, M. A. (2017). Engaging parents through better communication systems. *Educational Leadership, 75*(1), 58–62.

Kritikos, E. P., McLoughlin, J. A., & Lewis, R. B. (2018). *Assessing students with special needs* (8th ed.). Pearson.

Kuusisaari, H. (2014). Teachers at the zone of proximal development—Collaboration promoting or hindering the development process. *Teaching and Teacher Education, 43*, 46–57.

Lavian, R. H. (2013). "You and I will change the world": Student teachers' motives for choosing special education. *World Journal of Education, 3*(4), 10–25.

Liaupsin, C. J. (2015). Improving treatment integrity through functional approach to intervention support. *Behavioral Disorders, 41*(1), 67–76.

Lustig, M. W., & Koester, J. (2013). *Intercultural competence: Interpersonal communication across cultures* (7th ed.). Pearson.

Maheady, L., Zgliczynski, T., & Colón, G. (2019). Using flexible grouping. In J. McLeskey, L. Maheady, B. Billingsley, M. T. Brownell, & T. J. Lewis (Eds.), *High leverage practices for inclusive classrooms* (pp. 237–250). Routledge.

Marbley, A. F., Bonner, F., McKisick, S., Henfield, M. S., & Watts, L. M. (2007). Interfacing culture specific pedagogy with counseling: A proposed diversity training model for preparing preservice teachers for diverse learners. *Multicultural Education, 14*(3), 8–16.

Mariage, T., Winn, J., & Dabo, A. (2019). Provide scaffolded supports. In J. McLeskey, L. Maheady, B. Billingsley, M. T. Brownell, & T. J. Lewis (Eds.), *High leverage practices for inclusive classrooms* (pp. 197–214). Routledge.

Martin, J. N., & Nakayama, T. K. (2015). Reconsidering intercultural (communication) competence in the workplace: A dialectical approach. *Language & Intercultural Communication, 15*(1), 13–28.

Marx, T. A., Hart, J. L., Nelson, L., Love, J., Baxter, C. M., Gartin, B., & Schaefer Whitby, P. J. (2014). Guiding IEP teams on meeting the least restrictive environment mandate. *Intervention in School and Clinic, 50,* 45–50.

Matthews, W. J. (2003, Summer). Constructivism in the classroom: Epistemology, history and empirical evidence. *Teacher Education Quarterly, 30*(3),51–64.

McCullough, D. (1972). *The great bridge.* Simon & Schuster.

McLaughlin, M. J. (2012). Access for all: Six principles for principals to consider in implementing CCSS for students with disabilities. *Principal,* September/October, 22–26.

McLeskey, J., Maheady, L., Billingsley, B., Brownell, M. T., & Lewis, T. J. (2019). *High leverage practices for inclusive classrooms.* Routledge.

Minkel, J. (2017). Welcoming families by focusing on strengths. *Educational Leadership, 75*(1), 71–74.

Moll, L. C. (2006). *Vygotsky and education.* Cambridge University Press.

Murawski, W. W. (2015). Creative co-teaching. In W. W. Murawski & K. L. Scott (Eds.), *What really works in secondary education* (pp. 201–215). Corwin.

National Center on Intensive Intervention (2013, March). *Data-based individualization: A framework for intensive intervention.* American Institutes for Research. https://www.intensiveintervention.org/sites/default/files/DBI_Framework.pdf

National Education Association (2014). Positive behavioral interventions and supports: A multi-tiered framework that works for every student. https://www.nea.org/assets/docs/PB41A-Positive_Behavioral_Interventions-Final.pdf

Nelson, L. L. (2014). *Design and deliver: Planning and teaching using universal design for learning.* Brookes Publishing.

Nolet, V., & McLaughlin, M. J. (2005). *Accessing the general curriculum including students with disabilities in standards-based reform* (2nd ed.). Corwin Press.

O'Neill, R. E., Albin, R. W., Storey, K., Horner, R. H., & Sprague, J. R. (2015). *Functional assessment and program development for problem behavior: A practical handbook.* Cengage.

Osborne, A. G., & Russo, C. J. (2014). *Special education and the law: A guide for practitioners* (3rd ed.). Corwin Press.

Patton, J. R., & Trainor, A. (2002). Using applied academics to enhance curricular reform in secondary education. In C. A. Kochhar-Bryant & D. S. Bassett (Eds.), *Aligning transition and standards-based education: Issues and strategies* (pp. 55–75). Council for Exceptional Children.

Pierangelo, R. A., & Giuliani, G. (2017). *Assessment in special education: A practical approach* (5th ed.). Pearson.

Polloway, E. A., Epstein, M. H., & Bursuck, W. D. (2003). Testing adaptations in the general education classroom: Challenges and directions. *Reading and Writing Quarterly, 19*(2), 189–193.

Polloway, E. A., Patton, J. R., Serna, L., & Bailey, J. (2018). *Strategies for teaching learners with special needs* (11th ed.). Pearson.

Prince, A. M. T., Yell, M. L., & Katsiyannis, A. (2018). *Endrew F. v. Douglas County School District* (2017): The U.S. Supreme Court and special education. *Intervention in School & Clinic, 53*(5), 321–324. doi.org/10.1177/1053451217736867

Rao, K., & Meo, G. (2016). Using Universal Design for Learning to design standards-based lessons. *SAGE Open,* October–December, 6(4), 1–12. doi.org/10.1177/2158244016680688

Remillard, J. T. (2016). How to PARTNER with your CURRICULUM. *Educational Leadership, 74*(2), 34.

Salend, S .J. (2016). *Creating inclusive classrooms: Effective, differentiated, and reflective practices* (8th ed.). Pearson Education.

Samovar, L. A., Porter, R. E., McDaniel, E. R., & Roy, C. S. (2013). *Communication between cultures* (8th ed.). Wadsworth.

Samuels, C. A. (2017, October 25). Will ESSA reduce states' accountability in special ed? *Education Week, 37*(10), 19.

Samuels, C. (2018, January 24). Why special educators really leave the classroom: It's not just about paperwork, parents, and hard-to-manage students. *Education Week, 37*(18).

Schubert, W. H. (1993). Curriculum reform. In G. Cawelti (Ed.), *Challenges and achievements of American education* (pp. 80–112). Association for Supervision and Curriculum Development.

Shabani, K. (2016). Applications of Vygotsky's sociocultural approach for teachers' professional development. *Cogent Education, 3*(1), article 1252177. https://doi.org/10.1080/2 331186X.2016.1252177

Shannon, G. S., & Blysma, P. (2007). *Nine characteristics of high-performing schools: A research-based resource for schools and districts to assist with improving student learning* (2nd ed.). OSPI.

Shaw, S. F., & Madaus, J. W. (2008). Policy and law briefs: Preparing school personnel to implement Section 504. *Intervention in School and Clinic, 43*(4), 226–230.

Silverman, S. K., Hazelwood, C., & Cronin, P. (2009). *Universal education: Principles and practices for advancing achievement of students with disabilities.* Ohio Department of Education. education.ohio.gov/getattachment/Topics/School-Improvement/Ohio-Improvement-Process/Special-Education-Gap-Study.pdf.aspx

Sir, D. N. (2017). *Comparing two alternative assessments: Dynamic Learning Maps and Multi-state alternative assessment.* Unpublished doctoral dissertation. Seton Hall University. https:// eric.ed.gov/?id=ED581976

Sova, T., & Turcan, L. (2016). Empathy—A professional value of stress resistant teacher. *Bulletin of the Transilvania University of Brasov, 9*(58), 91–96.

Sprague, J.R., & Walker, H.M. (2005). *Safe and healthy schools: Practical prevention strategies.* Guilford Press.

Steinberg, J. (2014). An epistemic case for empathy. *Pacific Philosophical Quarterly, 95,* 47–71.

Sullivan, E., & Glidden, L. M. (2014). Changing attitudes towards disabilities through unified sports. *Intellectual & Developmental Disabilities, 52*(5), 367–378.

Swan, P., & Riley, P. (2015). Social connection: Empathy and mentalization for teachers. *Pastoral Care in Education, 33*(4), 220–230.

Thomas, S., & Dykes, F. (2011) Promoting successful transitions: What can we learn from RTI to enhance outcomes for all students? *Preventing School Failure, 55*(1), 1–9.

Tomlinson, C. A. (2001). *How to differentiate instruction in mixed-ability classrooms* (2nd ed.). Association for Supervision and Curriculum Development.

Tomlinson, C. A. (2014). *The differentiated classroom: Responding to the needs of all learners* (2nd ed.). Association for Supervision and Curriculum Development.

Tschannen-Moran, M., & Clement, D. (2018). Fostering more vibrant schools. *Educational Leadership, 75*(6), 28–33.

Turnbull, A., Turnbull, H. R., Erwin, E. J., Soodak, L. C., & Shogren, K. A. (2015). *Families, professionals, and exceptionality: Positive outcomes through partnership and trust* (7th ed.). Pearson.

Turnbull, A., Turnbull, H. R., Wehmeyer, M. L., & Shogren, K. A. (2013). *Exceptional lives: Special education in today's schools* (7th ed.). Pearson Education.

U.S. Department of Education. (2017, March 13). U.S. Secretary of Education Betsy DeVos Announces Release of Updated ESSA Consolidated State Plan Template. https://www. edu.gov/us-secretary-education-betsy-devos-announces-release-updated-essa-consolidated-state-plan-templat

Vaughn, S., & Bos, C. S. (2015). *Strategies for teaching students with learning and behavior problems* (9th ed.). Pearson.

Villegas, A. M., & Lucas, T. (2002). *Educating culturally responsive teachers: A coherent approach.* State University of New York Press.

Wehmeyer, M. L. (1996). Self-determination as an educational outcome: Why is it important to children, youth and adults with disabilities? In D. J. Sands & M. L. Wehmeyer (Eds.), *Self-determination across the life span: Independence and choice for people with disabilities* (pp. 17–36). Brookes.

Wiggins, G., & McTighe, J. (2005). *Understanding by design.* Association for Supervision and Curriculum Development.

Williams, B. (2001). *Adult learning theory: The mentoring connection.* University of Akron Press.

Wlodkowski, R. J., & Ginsberg, M. B. (1995). A framework for culturally responsive teaching. *Educational Leadership, 53*(1), 17–21.

Yell, M. L., & Drasgow, E. (2007). Assessment for eligibility under IDEIA and the 2006 regulations. *Assessment for Effective Intervention, 32*(4), 202–213.

Yell, M. L., Katsiyannis, A., Ennis, R. P., & Losinski, M. (2013). Avoiding procedural errors in individual education program development. *Teaching Exceptional Children, 46*(1), 56–64.

Index

SUBJECTS

About the Authors

Alice Tesch Graham is a professor of special education at Salve Regina University in Newport, RI. She holds a PhD in Special Education from the University of Florida and is a life-long special educator. Her career began teaching students in special education and serving as a cooperating teacher. For over 30 years Dr. Graham has worked in teacher preparation supporting the development of novice special educators through teaching coursework and supervising student teachers. She has presented extensively at conferences on the topics of service learning, collaboration, and teacher preparation in special education. Her teaching focus and research interests are on developing effective special educators and facilitating effective communication across various roles. Dr. Graham lives in Newport with her husband Will.

Gia Anselmo Renaud is currently an assistant professor of elementary and early childhood education at Bridgewater State University in Massachusetts, where she supervises student teachers and teaches courses in Sheltered English Immersion and inclusion. Prior to teaching at Bridgewater, Dr. Renaud spent 16 years teaching in both general and special education elementary classrooms in urban settings. She has presented at National Teacher Education Conferences on the topics of student teaching, collaboration, service learning and the use of mixed reality simulation with teacher candidates. Her research interests are social–emotional learning, including students with disabilities, and teacher preparation. Dr. Renaud resides in Somerset, MA, with her husband, Dennis, and daughter, Allison.

Martha McCann Rose is a professor in the Education Department at Salve Regina University, Newport, RI. Dr. Rose began her teaching career as a secondary English teacher. In her current position, she has taught in both the special education and secondary education programs. In addition, Rose is a fellow at The Pell Center for International Relations and Public Policy at Salve Regina University. Her international teaching has included providing professional development in Dehra Dun, India, and Santiago, Chile. Rose is the director of the Nuala Pell Leadership Program, which prepares students to work in the public sector. Her interests include international education, social and emotional learning, and working with English learners. Dr. Rose and her husband, Tom, divide their time between Newport and Washington, DC, where her daughter, son-in-law, and grandchildren reside.